Authority and Influence in Leadership

How to Lead, Negotiate, and Inspire in the Modern Workplace

Josh Macalinao

Contents

Introduction

P ower and authority serve necessary functions across organizations and societies. Hierarchies establish order amidst complexity through clearly delineated responsibilities and centralized decisions governing collective behaviors. Control provides efficiency where ambiguity risks dysfunction. Leaders occupying formal elevated roles rightfully claim heightened influence, as titles confer special privileges and obligations for steering institutional direction. Executives must wield significant power judiciously to uphold commitments towards multiple stakeholders depending profoundly on their judgment calls.

Yet unaccountable dominance risks distortion, as Lord Acton famously noted regarding corruption tending to accompany absolute power bereft of checks. From front line managers to celebrated CEOs, leadership miscues trace frequently to figures wielding authority absent balanced perspective. Overreliance upon positional prerogatives while underdeveloping softer skills of persuasion, empathy and accountability often yields disastrous impacts rippling through entire cultures.

Therefore, modern uncertainties increasingly require reliance upon more collaborative approaches from leaders ready to catalyze cooperation using tools of inspiration. Volatility and disruption demand nimble learning nervous systems over centralized organs sluggish to adapt. As yesterday's playbooks fade rapidly into obsolescence, progress relies on flattened, transparent architectures pooling dispersed insights into coordinated responses. And the fuel energizing such collective mobilization springs from influential leadership more than hierarchical power.

This emerging reality requires reimagining outdated mental models that equate leadership exclusively with formal authority rather than multifaceted capabilities blending positional privileges with personal influence. Certain formal powers always hold necessary utility. But applied absent countervailing forces, brute power tends towards abuse more frequently than ambitiously empowering teams. Therefore, the modern leader must pair formal capabilities with skillful persuasion that earns allies through passion and reason versus coercion and carrots. Progress manifests through enrolled participants, not obedient followers merely complying without understanding.

The Promise and Peril of Power

Hierarchy serves vital purposes across human organizations. Structures clarity responsibilities essential for complex coordination. Just as bodily health requires a controlling brain, institutions depend on leadership directing strategy and operations in service of shared goals. Senior authority figures claim heightened decision rights, resource control and prominent platforms based formally on rank. Followers cede certain freedoms to leaders in exchange for order and collective advancement.

And yet unquestioned power risks distortion. As institutions mature and leaders capture excessive privileges, assumptions go unchallenged and alternate perspectives excluded. Groupthink supplants diversity. And without transparency or accountability forcing continual reevaluation, decisions drift towards isolated interests rather than balancing stakeholder needs. Power's accompanying certainty of correctness obscures the necessity fordoubt, invitation and discovery.

At its worst extremes, raw power unrestrained entirely by competing influences devolves into outright totalitarian control focused obsessively on dominance itself rather than constructive outcomes. But well before such dire manifestations, power's tendency towards self-reinforcing conviction frequently yields suboptimal results and cultural harm across organizations. Fear-based coercion and rewards targeting narrow performance extract compliance at cost of ingenuity and allegiance. Force cannot replicate the dedication inspired through purpose.

These observations furnish no categorical indictment against formal authority itself when applied judiciously, but rather serve as caution towards unaccountable power's risks when not counterbalanced appropriately. Certain platforms and privileges hold indispensible utility for governance. Hierarchies create order amidst complexity. Strategic leaders must steer collective behaviors by deciding direction.
And yet leadership solely based on position ultimately limits potential by choking innovation and obscuring realities from above. Progress depends profoundly on influence deliberately decentralized across organizations to spark broad participation fused towards shared goals.

Therefore, sustainable thriving requires power balanced by persuasive influence skillfully applied towards earning allies rather than commanding subordinates. And influence proves most enduring when founded upon credibility from expertise, integrity and empathy. Visionaries enrolling teams through inspiration lead others because they first lead themselves through accountability and service. They wield authority not as iron fist, but as gentle shepherds convening talent towards possibility.

The Promise of Influence

Influence represents leadership's definitive source of exponential impact, determining the pace and scope of progress realizable when harnessed appropriately. While formal authority governs behaviors within narrowly defined organizational boundaries, influence expands possibilities by mobilizing discretionary efforts towards the improbable. Through tools of reason, passion and relationship building, influencers architect movements that spark chain reactions across vast networks. They transform solitary goals into mass pursuits by awakening human potential and infecting teams with a shared sense of purpose.

And unlike formal titles conferring power through credentials and appointments alone, influence must perpetually re-earn its legitimacy through expertise and relationships validated by followers themselves, not institutions. Demonstrated accountability builds foundational trust in a leader's capabilities and character. Consistently delivering results and supporting colleagues through challenges establishes reputational credibility that lends weight when championing ideas or steering discussions. Reliability generates authority. One leading indicator of rising influence involves subordinates beginning to emulate and perpetuate your behaviors, language and methodologies.

But cultivating committed disciples rather than merely dutiful employees requires engaging hearts, not just convincing minds through tactics of rational persuasion. Human beings ultimately commit loyalty not to impersonal bureaucracies and org charts but rather to causes and individuals resonating with inner identities and values. Effective influencers awaken latent creativity by framing progress as collaborative adventures rather than issuing rigid decrees. They customize calls appealing to diverse psychologies and talents. Through inquiry-based inspiration more than declarative direction, they enroll teams emotionally while granting flexibility for customization and mastery seeking. Ownership develops community and tenacity.

Additionally, positive influencers root appeals in concern for collective welfare, not self-interest. They focus first on understanding colleagues and customers on grounded human levels before seeking to be understood. Then they anchor ideas around shared priorities rather than dictating alternatives. Solutions spark participation when co-created, not delivered fully formed. Their pull invites voluntary followership.

Such inspiration demands authenticity. Influence leaders wield authority by walking their talk consistently and through tenure across challenges. They embody purpose in daily behaviors, liver their truth openly and demonstrate care beyond rhetoric. You cannot credibly call for standards you fail to uphold personally. Their ideals proved through actions recruit legions prepared to imitate excellence.

Therefore, while formal authority always maintains necessary utility, influence accrued through expertise, relationships and integrity offers far greater potential for elevating organizations. Power grasps the immediate but inspiration envision the impossible. Progress depends on integrating scattered strengths across teams inspired by purposeful visions they help shape. And sustainable futures arise through decentralized leadership fusing insights between authorities above seeing from altitude and frontliners below informed by ground proximity to changing realities. Flatter, open architectures outpace closed hierarchies when markets demand responsiveness.

The question before every leader thus becomes: will we cling to comforts of control or accept ambiguities of influence that depend profoundly on earning legitimacy repeatedly rather than operating on credentials or position? Can we ignite participatory cultures aligned through accountable influence more than singular vision? Progress may depend profoundly on how we answer the call...

Balancing Power and Influence

The preceding analysis clearly indicates fundamental tensions between leadership power tied to formal structure and influence amassed through expertise plus relationships that relies on continual validation. Power provides firmness but risks rigidity when applied dogmatically. Influence furnishes inspiration yet depends profoundly on consistent demonstration of accountable impact to sustain legitimacy. Neither holds a monopoly on best practices.

Rather, continuously recalibrating situational approaches based on balancing power's stability against influence's nimbleness offers highest probability paths for navigating perpetually dynamic challenges arising across organizations. Power plays strongest suit when urgency requires firm direction, such as during crises, structure building or executing repeatable operations at scale. But heavy-handed authority risks rebellion and chokes agility over time. Influence ignition unlocks discretionary passions by framing progress as participatory and meaning-rich, igniting grassroots innovation closer to the edge. But such volatility requires steadying through accountability and outcomes.

Therefore, determining ideal positioning along the combined continuum expressed as "direction versus participation" stands as the defining calculus for leadership excellence moving forward. And just as strategy and culture must fuse towards customer value, so too must influence and authority synthesize for institutions to progress. Neither flourishes in isolation. Visionaries enrolling allies through inspiration understand that formal power provides platforms for possibility. Influence gives flight to dreams that authority grounds in reality through accountable application of resources, metrics and priorities.

Bureaucracies no longer hold monopolies on wisdom in age when ground truths surface instantly online. But collectives lacking administration risk dysfunction's entropy. Therefore, leaders must judge contexts constantly to apply situational power through hierarchy or inspire progress through horizontal influence among peers. Centralized and decentralized models should coexist for organizations to harness stability with flexibility. Rather than power or influence alone, hybrid approaches distinguish exemplary leadership today.

And just as movies blend closeup camera intimacy with aerial establishing shots into compelling narratives, so too must influence and authority partner contextually to direct coordinated behaviors effectively across complex challenges. No individual harbors sufficient perspective alone to guarantee optimal choices in perpetually shifting environments. But collectively, fused insights unlock potential through shared possibilities.

Therefore, the path forward weaves wisdom centralized through formal power that grounds vision into implementable stratagems with creativity decentralized through informal collaborative influence sparking progress across dispersed complex systems. Structure enables while culture energizes. Neither dominates in isolation. Authority provides tools for cooperation at scale while inspiration furnishes fuel propelling innovation. Power and influence must dance together skillfully, each making room for the other.

The Heart of Great Leadership

Ultimately, neither titles nor skills furnish magic bullets universally guaranteeing leadership excellence. Formal authority and persuasive influence both carry situational utility when applied judiciously, but over-reliance on any singular approach risks imbalances as contexts and priorities perpetually evolve. Leadership requires wisdom - a word originating from deep seeing - to observe realities through grounded empathy and adapt in service of collective advancement rather than inflexible models or personal benefit. And that clarity of vision stems profoundly from leaders themselves focused first on developing sound character.

In this sense, leadership proves less science than art. Technical capabilities always matter but personal maturity matters more. Executives and administrators will only progress institutions as far as their developmental capacity stretches to carry complexity and uncertainty while upholding courage and compassion. Prominent thought leader Peter Drucker summarized this imperative for self-mastery succinctly: "Management is doing things right; leadership is doing the right things." Doing the right things - especially under duress - requires grounded ethical seeing.

Obsession with control or technique alone risks overlooking deeper human dimensions that provide the true drivers of culture and progress. Strategy only sets direction. Environment emerges based profoundly on whether participants feel sufficiently psychologically safe to create and take risks while operating interdependently at peaks of capability. And that security springs from leadership presence etched into every conversation and behavior - who they are communicates louder than whatever they declare. Titans focused on influence more than empathy fall flat when lacking emotional intelligence and self-awareness...a blindness all too common among those elevated on platforms high enough to lose sight of grounded reality from such dizzying altitudes. They simply cannot see their own limitations of perspective from atop aura-wrapped peaks. And this constraint holds dire implications in data rich era when ground truths permeate globally online long before trickling up traditional chains of offices.

Therefore, cultivating personal maturity represents the definitive penetration point for evolving leadership capabilities in disruptive times, when perpetual uncertainty demands resilience and continual learning. And maturation journeys require curiosity, courage and compassion as fundamental qualities that distinguish visionaries who transform versus those transfixed by visible constraints or social pressures. Curious leaders embody perpetual students embracing vulnerability while courage empowers the daring honesty to unravel discomforting truths. Great influencers remain dedicated always to lifting suppressed voices and concerns before those cracks rupture into catastrophic crises downstream. They transcend fears by expanding possibility paradigms that only open through seeking. With foundations of security established, creativity reigns.

Likewise, courage furnishes capacity to question constraints and dated assumptions reflection and risk reveal as suboptimal for current contexts. Bravery fuels disruptive innovation by anchoring experiments less in potential penalties suffered than benefits unlocked for multiplied stakeholders when tried-and-true playbooks fade into dysfunction. But daring dreams never shift norms alone. Catalyzing co-creators capable of translating vision into reality differentiates those who talk from those who transform.

Which illuminates leadership's definitive quality - compassion. For executive proclamations never become lived experience absent cultural adoption distributed across dispersed implementers. And what ultimately activates participation starts with emotional enrollment - appealing to hearts before heads and understanding intrinsic human needs central to engagement. People empower institutional purpose when assured contributory value will be honored beyond rhetoric. Belief follows belonging. With foundations of trust established through perceiving leaders' care for greater good - and faith they confront rather than shun harsh truths - ingenuity gets unleashed beyond constraints.

So there they stand - curiosity, courage and compassion. Leadership levers with exponential reach across relationships for reorienting assumptions and unleashing potential even amid seemingly impossible limitations like volatile markets, talent scarcities, bureaucratic inertia and skittish psychologies recoiling from the unfamiliar. But counterintuitively, visionaries guide teams successfully down uncharted paths by first calming minds through compassion while narrowing complexity into evaluable next actions through curiosity and courage. They transform dizzying uncertainty from inhibitor into inspiration and disrupt seemingly implacable obstacles by dissolving constraints exist largely as figments of perceptual limitation. Possibilities expand when the right leaders reshape beliefs through wisdom and trust.

But again,global visibility into leader behaviors demands alignment between values voiced and lived. One wrong action rings louder than years of strengths in era when ground observations permeate the internet. Therefore, continually earning credibility through integrity in crisis remains non-negotiable for influence retention across distrustful, wavering, high-performance teams. When environments shake, leaders calm by offering ballast through reliability plus self-aware stewardship more than positional authority. They withstand turbulence by championing mutual security transcendent of particular failures or misfortunes by coupling transparency with resiliency. And the resultant reputational halo effect furnishes immeasurable gravitational pull when engaging participants emotionally to attempt the improbable. But credibility fades fast without character - it rests profoundly on courageously continuing personal growth towards composure, empathy and wisdom applied situationally regardless of distractions bombardment. Inspiration fails where self-awareness lapses.

Therefore, leadership excellence emerges through balanced integration of formal capabilities, influence skills and personal mastery that blends curiosity, courage and compassion situationally upon fluid contexts. With humble learning as the core driver, progress unfolds one interaction at a time, continually re-earned through accountable impact. And across every organization, promise awaits activation in abundance - dispersed glimpses of alternative futures awaiting bold inquiry and connection into executable innovation. Realizing latent potential starts with leaders who calm turbulence by living integrity aloud. Their visions manifest as springboards for talent to perform unrestrained by fears of imperfection that inherently accompany risk. Psychological safety fuels breakthroughs where control fixation throttles creative output. Each of us occupies a leader's role empowered to uplift others in some capacity - whether through generosity of spirit, strength of example or platforms afforded by society. So accept that broadest definition by lifting those around you a bit higher each day through compassion, integrity and perpetual encouragement. Momentum builds behind the bold.

Now we stand equipped to commence applying insights from modern influence mastery and emotionally intelligent leadership towards architecting cultures of trust-based empowerment. With curiosity, courage and care as cornerstones, we are ready to start...

Chapter One

Understanding Power

Power manifests in various forms within the professional realm. While some leaders wield formal authority tied to their positions in a hierarchy, others draw influence from their personalities and social competencies. This alternative source of sway is known as personal power. Though more abstract than rank-derived might, it can prove equally potent in shaping workplace outcomes. By cultivating personal power, managers can positively impact their teams and organizations without relying solely on bestowed titles.

Within most companies, designated managers have been entrusted with formal decision-making capacity concerning their departments or staff members. By virtue of their job descriptions, these individuals can issue directives and expect compliance. Their authority stems from managerial status rather than any exceptional qualities innate to them as individuals. This external granting of control often minimizes the need for positional leaders to develop socially persuasive talents. However, overdependence on formal clout can inhibit flexibility and stifle innovation.

Alternatively, some leaders wield influence not from above but from within. Through determined self-cultivation of talents like empathy, integrity, and grit, these personal leaders inspire others to follow their vision. Their power emerges organically from coworkers' recognition of their exceptional drive, ethics, communication abilities or other standout qualities. Teams coalition around these leaders because they choose to, not because they have to. Needless dependency on hierarchy for workplace coordination becomes less necessary.

Blending Positional and Personal Power

Ideal leadership blends formal decision-making duties with the capacity to motivate voluntarily based on character. Managers should aim to develop both forms of influence rather than leaning too heavily on one or the other. Doing so will likely require consistent self-assessment and improvement.

What specific talents and traits contribute to personal leadership? While innate charisma can provide an early edge, most socially persuasive capabilities can be honed with commitment. Emotional intelligence, integrity, confidence without arrogance, authenticity, creative problem-solving and communication talents all help comprise personal power. Additionally, leaders should exude positivity. This uplifting energy inspires teams to push past self-interested concerns toward unified goals.

Keys to Unlocking Your Personal Power

If seeking to enhance personal leadership, consider the following suggestions:

Pursue self-mastery: Clarify your values, principles, strengths and weaknesses through routine reflection. Set aligned personal goals. Commit to lifelong betterment across mental, physical, social and spiritual domains. Self-actualized leaders radiate authenticity and operate from a place of inner conviction.

Hone emotional intelligence: Learn to identify subtle social dynamics among teams while remaining aware of your own emotional patterns. Refine abilities to express empathy, resolve tensions, and rally others around shared purpose. Leadership is fundamentally about social coordination.

Communicate vision persuasively: Storytelling talents distinguish inspiring leaders. Weave themes of authenticity and service into your vision while painting a vivid, hopeful picture of accomplishments ahead. Adapt messaging tone and complexity to connect uniquely with each listener.

Emphasize follower empowerment: Position yourself not as a hero but as a coach guiding others toward actualizing their own latent talents in service of collective victory. Framing leadership as a journey of group actualization defuses self-interested behavior among teams.

While formal authority certainly confers some advantages, leaders should resist overdependence on their job titles. Harnessing personal power generates flexibility to influence within and beyond hierarchical constraints. Blend formal and informal influence to unlock leadership potential.

Cultivating Personal Influence as a Leader

Leadership depends as much on inward drive as outward authority. While formal organizational hierarchies confer decision-making power to individuals in key roles, genuine influence ultimately springs from personal qualities like integrity, vision, and social mastery. As the stoic philosopher Seneca noted, "Most powerful is he who has himself in his own power." By cultivating their talents from within, leaders can enhance their capacity to motivate and coordinate teams.

This internal source of persuasion is known as personal power. It emerges not from job titles or ranks but from a leader's character. Personal power comprises traits that naturally inspire confidence, camaraderie and voluntary deference from peers. It flows from self-awareness, emotional intelligence, communicating vision, and leading by uplifting example. This influence is earned, not bestowed. Understanding and developing personal power empowers leaders to impact organizations with or without formal authority.

Two Wells of Personal Power: Referent vs. Expert

Personal power comes in two primary forms: referent and expert power. Referent power is the ability to connect, inspire and build rapport through personality strengths like charisma, approachability and public speaking talent. When we are drawn to someone because of their vision, empathy or optimism, they are exercising referent power. Think of iconic influencers like Martin Luther King Jr. or Steve Jobs. Their stirring speeches moved millions by force of passion, not formal orders.

Expert power also motivates from within but through deep knowledge rather than personal magnetism. When recognized as having mastery within a field, others seek out expert leaders for skilled guidance. Fellow engineers at Apple, for example, deferred to Steve Wozniak's technical wizardry during critical product development challenges.

While *referent power* moves people's hearts and expert power their minds, combining both can profound impact organizations. Still, leaders need not exhibit both to wield personal influence. Some may inspire more through humility and service rather than charisma. Others lead by marshaling knowledge rather than delivering gut-wrenching speeches. Further, overdependence on a single strength can produce imbalance, as when abrasive yet brilliant leaders breed anxiety. Discover your own authentic personal powers, but remember that leadership is a team effort. Surround yourself with complements.

Cultivating an Internal Locus of Control

While intrinsic leadership traits provide a foundation, personal power ultimately stems from self-mastery and believing one can overcome external barriers. Psychologists describe this mentality as having an "internal locus of control." Rather than seeing themselves as passive victims of circumstance, internally-powered leaders feel empowered to assign meaning to events and pivot situations toward desired outcomes.

Studies show that bosses and entrepreneurs skewed toward internal loci of control thrive even amid adversity. Setbacks become opportunities for growth rather than causes for resignation. Maintaining this mindset requires emotional self-regulation and refusing victim mentalities whenever challenges arise. Daily habits like reflection, vision-setting, exercising agency in small matters, and assuming full responsibility for mistakes also help internalize power.

The alternative "external locus of control" abandons influence to environmental or social factors. Such powerlessness quickly devolves into learned helplessness. Unfortunately, organizations sometimes incentivize this by concentrating decision authority only in upper management rather than empowering initiative from all levels. Flatter organizational models help combat this by spreading leadership responsibility across diverse teams. Fostering an internal locus of control organization-wide unlocks tremendous discretionary effort and performance gains.

Putting Personal Power to Work

While referent and expert power provide means for influence, internal locus determines the strength of one's motivational muscles. How precisely can rising leaders begin applying personal power to benefit their organizations?

Start from within. Regularly reflect on your principles, strengths, growth areas and vision. Set aligned development goals. Model the ethic of continual improvement you wish to see organizationally.

Next, diligently expand emotional intelligence. How do staff members respond to your leadership style and communication choices? Set a positive emotional tone by remaining aware of morale. Reshape any tendencies toward impatience or poor empathy.

Also, compellingly communicate vision instead of just issuing directives. Share authentic stories that spark others' passions. Appeal to hearts as well as minds. Frame work as a journey toward service and actualization.

Additionally, establish trust by welcoming pushback. Critique does not represent insubordination but rather genuine dialogue. Foster psychological safety among teams where all feel valued contributors.

Finally, transfer formal authority to those below through encouragement and development. Your purpose as a leader is to unleash latent talents in service of shared goals. Share credit abundantly and avoid control tendencies.

While positional power has its advantages, personal influence gains you more. Leadership is not a solo endeavor but rather a social energizing process. Enrich your personal powers in order to empower those around you

Understanding and Applying the 7 Types of Positional Authority

Leadership is profoundly shaped by how power gets distributed and applied within teams. While personal talents and traits contribute, managers also leverage authority tied directly to their formal roles. This capacity to influence others based on positional status is known as positional power. Sound leadership requires applying the right types properly.

Positional influence comes in seven primary varieties, each with distinct pros and cons. As mapped by the influential French-Raven framework, these include:

1. Legitimate Power

2. Coercive Power

3. Reward Power

4. Expert Power

5. Informational Power

6. Connection Power

7. Referent Power

Below we will explore the essence of each type of authority, when appropriately (or inappropriately) applied, and how these powers intermingle in practice. Wise leaders understand that overdependence on certain types can undermine organizational health. Blending influences fluidly based on context separates truly visionary managers from mere taskmasters.

Legitimate Power: The Authority You're Handed

Formal leadership roles confer decision-making capacity known as legitimate power. Board directors, executive managers, department heads - all wield hierarchical clout over their respective teams. Legitimate power manifests through actions like hiring, budget allocation, strategy setting and finalizing projects. Employees comply based on acknowledgment of granted oversight.

However, while such positional authority establishes necessary order, overreliance fosters dysfunction. Legitimate power requires balance with less rigid influences like inspiration and expertise. Savvy leaders reserve hierarchical leverage only for course corrections when alternative forms of guidance fail. They also frame leadership as service rather than unilateral control. Wise stewards understand all power originates from below, not above.

Coercive Power: Avoid Brute Intimidation

In contrast to legitimate authority's rightful duty, coercive power leads through brute intimidation. Rather than earning buy-in, coercive leaders demand performance under threats of disciplinary action or termination. Their tool is naked fear rather than consent. Unfortunately, some mistake such domineering for strength much as victims of abuse tragically cling to notion of love.

Yet despite its continued prevalence, studies confirm coercive power reliably diminishes organizational performance along with employee well-being. Leaders relying on threats and micromanagement to extract compliance from teams breed anxiety and learned helplessness. Both productivity and creativity inevitably suffer.

The rare context warranting disciplinarian scare tactics demands immediate crisis intervention, not sustained behavioral change. Even there, coercive power risks embittering teams toward formal leadership. Bewarebrute intimidation's temptations. As legends like Gen. George S. Patton attest, gallantry inspires where terror reduces cowering peasants. Guess which multiply an army's might?

Reward Power: Motivate Through Incentives

Savvier leaders lure superior performance through reward power's positive reinforcements. Provides like pay raises, promotions, extra time off and verbal recognitions tap our innate drive to better our conditions. Within human capital limits, such incentivization elicits discretionary effort from workers otherwise content meeting minimal expectations.

Yet incentives alone fail to nurture high-functioning teams. Once accustomed to transactional leadership cultures fixated on tit-for-tat bartering, personnel reduce delivering excellence to calculating returns on personal investment. Intrinsically purpose-driven effort gets crowded out by self-interest. Leaders must spark passion through compelling vision layered atop extrinsic motivations.

Informational Power: The Knowledge You Have

Information is power. Project managers armed with data required for key decisions can influence team direction despite lacking formal authority. This informational power sways by limiting options. However, exclusive gatekeeping of intelligence for personal advantage risks fostering resentment and distrust. Savvy leaders demonstrate transparency.

Still, certain confidential matters concerning internal company information, customer data or acquisition plans warrant discretion. There, informational power rightfully provides temporary influence until details become public.

Otherwise, fluid information sharing not only earns respect but unlocks synergistic potential. Suppressed ideas steward continued ignorance. For inspirational leadership, data empowers the many, not the few.

Expert Power: Follow the Thought Leader

While informational power discloses facts, expert power leverages the acumen to interpret them. Subject matter authorities shape team direction by force of superior mastery. For technical guidance, trusted specialists merit greater sway. We rightfully defer on matters of human health to physicians rather than risk amateurish misdirection.

Yet even here, credible leaders exhibit humility by welcoming scrutiny of their guidance. Blind obedience to proclaimed expertise risks groupthink vulnerabilities and ethical breaches. Once secured through demonstrated excellence, expert power must continue earning validation rather than retreating behind credentials. Continual learning sustains followings. Otherwise the erstwhile top gun flounders when leapfrogged by hungrier upstarts.

Connection Power: Your Allies in Influence

Authority also flows through proxy via connection power. By forging direct access to decision-maker ears, persuasive deputies bypass rigid hierarchies to shape outcomes. Such political channel tapping can navigate obstructionist barriers otherwise bottlenecking progress. Yet overreliance breeds toxic glad-handing and clawing sycophancy.

Effective leaders therefore minimize power plays founded solely on personal alliance making. Fair consideration and role-aligned authority should determine whose voices steer direction, not private access. Otherwise organizational health suffers from closed loop idea reinforcement apart from ground truths. However, certain intractable scenarios require working influences indirectly through trust agents. There, connection power assists.

Referent Power: Lead by Example

Referent power shapes through earned admiration, not formal rank. When embodied ideals like passion, integrity and service resonate as worthy models for emulation, followers coalesce organically behind moral leaders they revere. Such inspiration uplifts ordinary achievement into extraordinary devotion. Teams yearn to actualize the vision personified by their guiding light.

Yet for referent authority to empower beyond fleeting fervor, conduct must align with message. As models for imitation, leaders must personify their own soaring rhetoric. When hypocrisy erupts through unchecked egotism or ethical lapses, disillusionment breeds cynicism rather than fueling excellence. Those who would lead must live the change they wish to see. For noble hearts with eyes fixed horizonal, progress follows.

The above powers mingle in application but each warrants matching context and dosage. Overemphasis of one over others risks imbalance. Master fluid transitions between authority types and progress flows. Such wisdom separates truly visionary leaders from shortsighted opportunists. Take care therefore in how influence gets exerted within teams. For with authority comes great responsibility. How will you lead?

Balancing Power with Accountability

"With great power comes great responsibility." This maxim rings eternally true, yet history brims with examples of unchecked authority bred by toxic organizational cultures. Dominance intoxicates. Privilege blinds. In too many cases, emboldened leaders wield might without care for those impacted, causing real damage. However, ethical leaders understand that power and responsibility remain inseparable. They hold themselves accountable through perpetual self-reflection, feedback gathering, integrity cultivation and team empowerment. For with influence comes obligation to those granting such privilege in the first place.

Quieting Ego to Hear Hard Truths

Prominent leaders often surround themselves with praise singers verifying pre-existing biases rather than issuing necessary critiques. The trappings of success - be they mansions, yes men or perhaps just corner offices - isolate top executives from ground truths. Remaining rooted requires what the ancient Greeks called a "truth teller" or parrhesiastes to keep egos in check.

Reputational accountability therefore necessitates identifying at least one trusted, impartial advisor willing to spotlight difficult issues without repercussion. Regularly quiet internal noise to hear hard but caring transparency from such friends or partners. Install processes welcoming upward feedback from all levels. Left unchecked, dominance breeds ignorance and abuse. With power comes required obligation to continually validate direction.

Integrity's Halo Protects Reputations

Increased visibility also intensifies reputational risk from ethical lapses. The Information Age's transparency leaves little hidden for long, especially for prominent leaders. While establishments have traditionally shielded abuses of power fromExposure, such smokescreens now rarely survive scandals.

Therefore,exemplary character matters more than ever in an era where salacious headlines travel globally overnight. Personal integrity casts a halo protectingor alternately shatteringprofessional brands instantly. Board rooms and customers today examine leaders as representatives of their company's values, not just financial stewards. Upholding principles demonstrates accountability.

Empowering Teams Instills Ownership Culture

Power also obligates through responsible team development. Rather than controlling direction through authority alone, accountable leaders transfer ownership downward by empowering personnel to manage roles themselves. This distributes accountability across an organization rather than concentrating influence solely in executives.

Studies confirm that fostering autonomy optimizes engagement, performance ownership and innovation from below. In contrast, micromanagement and strict control may extract compliance but rarely excel beyond satisfactory effort minimums. For conscientious leaders, responsibility includes unlocking others' potential by granting authority to match. Empowered teams display greater initiative accountability.

Owning Commitments Earns Trust

Additionally, reputations depend heavily on consistently following through on obligations large and small. Leaders who habitually overcommit yet underdeliver erode critical trust from peers and personnel. Promiscuous pledging followed by flimsy excuses trains teams to discount future assurances. Lost confidence impairs initiatives relying on communal buy-in.

Combat such credibility corrosion by tracking commitments, breaking intimidating goals into stepwise milestones, delegating through clarity, and regularly reviewing progress toward deliverables with stakeholders. Reliability demonstrates accountability even more than talent ever could. For with authority comes obligation to uphold words matching the vision cast.

Conscientious Cultures Discourage Domination

Instilling accountability organization-wide minimizes abusive tendencies from coagulating power behind closed doors. Reviews prioritizing ethics tighten institutional pressures against inappropriate conduct from atop lofty perches. Establish open escalation channels welcoming input from all levels.

Set the tone from the top down through transparency, candid dialogue, eliminating unnecessary hierarchy and calling out indifference. Stress communal obligation over personal privilege. Guide gently and people will follow farther than any authority could otherwise compel. For responsibility fosters far greater devotion than fear.

While influence brings temptation toward exploitation, conscientious leaders remain grounded in accountability to those granting such authority. They validate direction through consistent feedback solicitation, safeguard reputations by upholding stringent ethics, transfer ownership downward via autonomy and reinforce reliability by honoring commitments. For with great power comes greater obligation to exercise such privilege only for others' benefit rather than personal gain. Lead accountably. Progress then naturally follows your lead.

Key Takeaways and Final Thoughts on Understanding Power

Key Takeaways:

- Personal power, derived from qualities like integrity and social mastery, complements formal authority in effective leadership. Cultivate talents boosting your capacity to connect, inspire and earn others' voluntary support.

- Blend formal duties with personal powers fluidly. Overreliance on one over the other causes imbalance. Know when hierarchical direction works and when inspiration better mobilizes.

- Develop an internal locus of control. See setbacks as growth opportunities rather than causes for victimhood. Take full ownership for all outcomes experienced.

- Employ positional power types judiciously. While legitimate authority brings necessary order, overuse breeds dysfunction. Avoid coercion's harms. Sparingly apply sticks and carrots.

- Continually re-earn validation rather than resting on credentials or alliances. Seek frequent feedback. Demonstrate accountability through reliability and transparency.

- Transfer influence downward by empowering teams through autonomy. Trusted talent accepts responsibility rather than requiring micromanagement. Foster communal ownership.

- With privilege comes obligation to self-reflect, safeguard reputations, elevate others and uphold commitments. The more influence exerted, the greater one's responsibility to handle power carefully.

Power & Influence

Leadership confers heavy responsibilities upon those elevated to formal or informal positions of influence. Executives, managers, experts and revered influencers all affect lives through their decisions and conduct. Followers entrust authority figures with precious talents, time, and trust. Yet dominance risks distortion if not handled carefully.

As explored throughout this chapter, power requires diligent accountability to avoid abuses. Through tactics like continual self-reflection, transparency, integrity cultivation and team empowerment, conscientious leaders uphold their obligations to those granting them influence. They grasp that authority originates from below, not above.

Might makes not right. While hierarchies establish order, coercion more often hinders than helps. Control fixations choke innovation. Thus visionaries lead by inspiration's lift not fear's gravity. They persuade through expertise and idealized example. People follow first because they trust, only then obey.

Does influence obligate? Unequivocally, yes. But dutiful service supports more than heavy-handed rule ever could. So handle leadership privileges with care. Directors are but stewards of talent entrusted to their care by human hearts yearning for actualization. Tend that spark, and progress follows.

What norms will govern your leadership? How will you leverage influence while maintaining humanity? May wisdom guide your path.

Chapter Two

Understanding Influence

Effective leadership in today's evolving business landscape requires much more than formal authority or position power. With flattening organizational structures, cross-functional project teams, and increased workforce mobility, even high-ranking executives find it challenging to drive change solely from the top down. Now more than ever, leaders must complement their hard power with soft power by mastering the art of influence.

As management guru John C. Maxwell famously stated, "Leadership is influence - nothing more, nothing less." But what does it really mean to influence others, and how can savvy professionals expand their influence to lead teams and organizations to shared success? This guide explores four proven methods of influence tailored for the modern workplace.

The Power of Persuasion Through Reasoned Arguments

Persuasion relies on logic and factual evidence to show that a requested course of action makes good sense. Unlike commanding by decree, persuasion explains why a particular decision or initiative will benefit the organization and individual employees alike. For instance, a tech company CEO persuades skeptical department heads that migrating servers to the cloud will boost security, reduce costs, and allow IT teams to focus on more innovative projects. She presents real-world case studies from competitors detailing how cloud adoption accelerated speed-to-market for new products. And she offers one-on-one sessions to address any security or budget concerns. This thoughtful approach wins over critics through rational arguments.

The Collaborative Power of Commitment and Inclusion

Savvy leaders tap into collaboration by soliciting ideas and input from the very people they seek to influence. When employees become active contributors rather than passive participants, they gain a shared sense of ownership and are more motivated to ensure the project's success. Facilitating collaborative workgroups across functions is especially impactful. It increases employee engagement while also exposing colleagues to new perspectives. Imagine a high-pressure initiative to improve customer response times is floundering. A unit head could issue demands for workers to increase productivity or face consequences. Or he could establish a cross-departmental process excellence team to study pain points and develop recommendations. Employees would appreciate the opportunity to shape solutions related to their day-to-day work.

The Inspirational Power of Role Modeling Desired Mindsets and Behaviors

Walking the walk beats talking the talk when it comes to inspiration. Leadership teams set the tone for organizational culture and performance expectations. So executives hoping to spark innovations or strengthen client relationships among frontline supervisors should start by modeling creativity themselves. Likewise, promoting greater collaboration and accountability means replacing siloed work habits with cross-functional knowledge sharing. Leaders telegraph intended changes through their own observable behaviors which cascades down through the ranks. Eventually, the new mindset manifests across all levels. But the process begins at the top, relying more on inspiration than proclamation.

The Consultative Power of Tapping Collective Wisdom

Consultation leverages employees' insights and experiences to shape consequential decisions before they are finalized. Some leaders consider seeking wide input to be inefficient or even threatening to their authority. Conversely, those who regularly consult staff view them as an invaluable intelligence resource that heightens commitment once plans are made. Imagine senior officials who need to formulate new customer service protocols ahead of a product launch. Internal surveys could inform initial proposals which then undergo review in focus group workshops. Representatives from sales, engineering and customer support would provide constructive critiques based on dealing with clients daily. This upfront reality-checking prevents executives from devising policies in a vacuum possibly misaligned from consumer expectations.

In truth, most leadership challenges rarely boil down to binary choices between wielding hard authority or soft persuasion. Situations calling for substantial organizational change often require wielding the right influence strategy at the right time. Bureaucratic cultures may first need directive declarations of shifting priorities from the C-suite before entertaining collaborative discussions or role model inspiration further down. Yet the most versatile leaders gradually phase towards influence techniques built on reasoning and engagement. This earns support through transparency while activating the collective wisdom within a workforce to drive change. Influence ultimately transcends any single technique by knowing which approach fits a given context or audience. Those able to persuasively communicate vision, actively involve team members and lead by example will discover their position power considerably amplified. But it starts with a mindset fixed on influencing rather than ordering.

Driving change in today's climate calls for rallying entire organizations around shared objectives. Leaders must look beyond position authority and learn the language of influence fluent in persuasion, collaboration, inspiration and consultation. Those that master these essential skills can transform individual convictions into collective actions through commitment instead of compliance.

The above framework provides critical building blocks but influencing also requires spending as much time listening as proclaiming. Leadership is dialogue, not monologue after all. With an open and engaging style combined with thoughtful influence strategies, progress unfolds one collaborative conversation at a time.

6 Strategies for Building Influence

Grasping influence in any organization hinges less on job titles than on seizing opportunities to guide teams toward meaningful transformations. Creative destruction has accelerated across industries where visionaries identify unmet needs then realign entire business models toward service enhancements over marginal improvements. Yet influence remains elusive, even for executives in the C-suite lacking strategies to rally colleagues, dismantle siloes and demonstrate readiness amid uncertainty. Mastery of several key areas separates those able to spur progress versus simply administer it. This chapter explores practical approaches for taking charge rather than passively holding positions. Concepts covered equip professionals at any level to:

- Formulate ambitions tied to customer-focused innovation versus status quo upkeep

- Take ownership through ideas, talent and resources that displace outdated conventions

- Build cooperative networks that bypass bureaucratic bottlenecks

- Seize leadership openings that arise amid crises, conflicts and uncertainty

- Focus battles only around defending essentials like budgets and talent

While rapid evolutions in technology and globalization reward bold new trajectories, influence accelerates their adoption through united human efforts. The following framework prepares any driven professional to shape an organization's path meaningfully regardless of title.

Leading with Ambition and Vision

True influence stems from bold yet attainable visions for growth. Leaders in business do more than just maintain operations - they guide teams and organizations to places they could not reach alone. Consider legendary conquests like Alexander the Great, who built an empire spanning three continents. His relentless ambition stands the test of time. Your own vision need not entail such epic scope, but must challenge teams beyond their comfort zone. Incremental goals barely ripple the status quo when disruptive innovations rewrite entire industries. Channel ambitious plans into uniting colleagues behind a distinctly better future, rendered in clear milestones. Allow them to see their contributions accelerating transformations once deemed impossible. With clarified direction, progress unfolds one committed step after the next.

Taking Charge Through Ideas, People and Purpose

However, heartfelt visions lose force without the plans, talents and resources behind it. Many managers occupy positions of authority without truly leading. They oversee operations originally built by others and follow precedents no longer suited to shifting marketplace demands. Leadership means grasping the reins to guide your organization along new routes that serve current challenges. This hinges on taking charge rather than idly holding a title. Build momentum by first formulating ideas to usher in a more competitive era. Then rally the team whose skills and mindsets best fit that vision. Lastly secure budgets that fuel execution. Remember that appropriations chase compelling ideas supported by capable individuals more than the reverse. Financials must align with goals of course but money alone cannot spark and sustain transformations. With clear ideas, well matched teams and affordably funded initiatives, progress unfolds one decision at a time.

Cultivating Connections that Support Your Goals

routing visions through rigid hierarchies or siloed departments invites delay or dilution. Every business encompasses networks of formal and informal influence among decision makers. Even where formal powers concentrate at the executive level, trusted advisors often sway outcomes prior to official decrees. Therefore cultivate connections spanning key leaders and supporting staff in roles like Finance, HR and IT. Their capacity to veto initiatives warrants as much care as charming superiors. Consider these gatekeepers as partners rather than obstacles. Getting to know them helps simplify processes later on. Communicate respectfully about how your plans align with company objectives. Dialogue around shared interests makes securing approvals easier especially when resources fall short. With open channels of communication, progress unfolds one cooperative relationship at a time.

Seizing Opportunities to Demonstrate Leadership

Adherence to hierarchy means waiting for those at the top to designate you as a leader. But moments arise outside this structure to distinguish your readiness and earn influence organically. Crises, conflicts, uncertainty and new initiatives all involve decisions that shape events well before official statements do. Where many recoil from turmoil, step forward with level-headed guidance aligned to organizational priorities. For instance, spearhead solutions, not fault-finding, amidst sudden misfortunes. Frame disagreements around constructive debate not personal attacks. Dispel ambiguity through pragmatic tests rather than paralysis by analysis. Help launch change by aligning innovations to strategic roadmaps. Each juncture to calmly direct stakeholders outpaces weeks of vying for leadership appointments. With every situation addressed thoroughly, progress unfolds one opportunity at a time.

Fighting Only When You Must

Of course, force of will alone fails to guarantee you steer the organization's course single-handedly. Opposition appears at times no matter how compelling the vision or coalitions formed. But rather than waging war over minor turf or stylistic differences, know precisely when a public stand protects progress.

Fight selectively around defending budgets, assignments, resources and personnel needed to achieve results. Even then, use logic and transparency versus hostility to state your case. Keep conflicts focused completely on practical needs not bruised egos. With astute judgment, progress unfolds through productive partnerships not needless clashes.

Today's complex business landscape demands leaders able to see beyond quarterly forecasts toward long term transformations meaningful for customers and colleagues alike. Executives who take charge, build connections and demonstrate readiness position organizations to meet that calling. While no single skillset guarantees smooth reception of bold ideas, incorporate the framework above and your influence will grow commensurate to your elevated vision.

Leading Through Influence

Command and control structures dominated management mindsets throughout the 20th century industrial economy centered on stability over agility. Rigid hierarchies relied on authority flowing from the top down based on formal titles rather than real-world capabilities. However, accelerating technological and economic shifts have exposed the shortcomings of authoritarian leadership styles. Innovations emerge rapidly across markets where nimble startups reshape entire industries nearly overnight. Legacy corporations saddled with inflexible chains of command often find themselves disrupted before they can pivot effectively. Now more than ever, organizations must replace old assumptions that employees simply require orders with frameworks that inspire ownership. Leading through influence represents the new imperative for unlocking potential within teams and colleagues themselves.

The Power of Inspiration Over Oversight

Managers adhering to outdated traditions depend on obedience compelled through official rankings like "vice president" or "director." They issue directives based on where they sit on an organization chart instead of earning followership by demonstrating sound judgement and inclusive decision-making. Short-term compliance occurs under threat of consequences but performance suffers over time through disengaged workers merely going through the motions. Conversely, influential leaders cultivate buy-in by connecting professional growth to corporate success. They paint a vivid vision of achievements possible when united by shared purpose rather than simply maximizing quarterly profits. Highlighting how innovations enhance customer experiences proves more inspirational than citing figures from an annual report. Savvy influencers also boost participation by delegating authority across cross-functional teams versus concentrating power at the top. As global pioneer of decentralized organizations Ricardo Semler discovered, "When you trust people they respond by giving you more to trust them with."

Communication That Empowers Beyond Instructions

Bureaucratic managers interact largely through issuing instructions down the chain of command. They expect compliance rather than engagement, silencing constructive debate that uncovers operational barriers. However, research confirms that influence strongly correlates to open and empathetic communication styles that dismantle walls between leaders and staff. Effective influencers seek regular input through circulated surveys, collaborative task forces and skip-level meetings with frontline personnel. Welcome questions and contrary opinions get raised early on instead of erupting as resistance later. Transparent discussions around aligning individual development goals to corporate objectives encourages accountability rooted in growth rather than consequences. Even when hard choices involve downsizing or restructuring, showing how it strengthens the overall organization long term earns support. By empowering people through candid and compassionate communication, progress unfolds through shared dedication, not grudging compliance.

Role Modeling Desired Culture From the Top

Hypocrisy breeds resentment faster than any authoritarian decree according to leadership experts. When superiors ask for behaviors they fail to demonstrate themselves, influence fades almost instantly. For example, expecting dedication through 60 hour work weeks from managers making family time a priority erodes trust. However, leaders who role model the mindsets they wish to propagate inspire adoption at all levels. Want more innovation? Give recognition to an employee expanding beyond their formal responsibilities. Seek better collaboration? Shoot down siloed thinking by hosting cross departmental lunches to share challenges and ideas. Prioritize diversity and inclusion? Call out and counteract any observed microaggressions immediately. Setting the tone at the top establishes real instead of empty values. With visible alignment, influence amplifies as participants at all levels act in concert.

The Competitive Advantages of Empowerment

The command and control model once sufficient in slowly evolving markets shows strain under unrelenting pace of technological disruptions today. Adaptation happens at startups with flat structures and decentralized leadership rather than legacy corporations beholden to hierarchical procedures. Yet organizations need not choose between agility and scale. Digital transformations make possible flexible teams empowered to bypass bureaucratic bottlenecks when addressing client demands or marketplace opportunities. The most prominent firms already invest heavily in upskilling workforces for maximum autonomy through reskilling programs. This underlies the rise of employee experience officers at large companies seeking to attract and retain top talent. Workers, especially millennials and Gen Zers, increasingly favor employers providing ongoing development opportunities above all else. Empowerment further drives retention when coupled with inspirational purpose. Data shows turnover falling up to 50% at firms able to communicate mission and meaning.

Elevating Leadership for the Age of Agility

Market volatility and technological disruption will only intensify as innovations create new sectors while reshaping existing ones. This points to influence as the differentiating leadership capability for organizational resilience moving forward. Structures must flatten to permit rapid responses without passing through endless channels of approval. Communicate for transparency and empathize across hierarchies more attuned to algorithms than egos. Making inspiration the incentive over authority gains immense leverage for securing buy-in. And as empowered team members reciprocate through greater trust and capability, enterprise wide agility follows. In truth, genuine influence wields commitment beyond compliance. People accord significant discretionary effort to leaders who respect and develop them while conveying purpose. Organizations that elevate staff in this way unlock unlimited potential.

Key Takeaways and Final Thoughts on Understanding Influence

Key Takeaways

- Influence stems from inspiring teams toward meaningful progress, not just holding titles

- Take charge by having big ideas, the right talent, and focused budgets

- Build networks to bypass bureaucratic bottlenecks

- Seize leadership opportunities during uncertainty

- Fight only to defend essential resources like budgets

Elevating Leadership Through Influence

Influence represents the modern imperative for organizational agility over rigid hierarchy. Market volatility and technological disruption reward flatter, faster-moving structures communicating vision through transparency versus edicts. As innovations reshape sectors, progress unfolds most swiftly when participants choose to commit talents toward shared missions rather than simply comply with superiors. This closing section summarizes key insights from our exploration of influence as the differentiating leadership capability moving forward.

Beyond steady-state oversight, influential leaders guide teams to places they could not reach alone. They set distinctly better futures rendered in clear milestones. Big, bold ambitions demand more than marginal gains but unlock discretionary efforts from talent seeking to transform entire industries. With clarified direction, progress unfolds one committed step after the next even amidst uncertainty. But significant influence requires grounding lofty visions through calculated execution.

Budgets chase compelling ideas supported by capable champions more than the reverse. Securing robust funding matters little absent an animating focus to deploy assets. Establish a strategic platform through customer-centric innovation before harnessing technology or appropriations. Then recruit and develop teams suited to see ambitions through from imagination to reality. With inspired personnel unified behind worthy endeavors, securing means follows. True influence wields human capital before financial capital.

No enterprise operates as a true hierarchy except perhaps onCoporate org charts. Authority resides across formal and informal networks governing decisions through criteria beyond rank. Obtaining buy-in requires viewing gatekeeping departments like IT, HR and Finance as collaborators versus adversaries even where friction emerges. Shared understanding shrinks downstream delays. With open channels of communication, progress unfolds one cooperative relationship at a time.

Market turbulence will only intensify across sectors and geographies, rewarding organizations agile enough to adapt. But what enables genuine agility? Structures and systems carry weight but ultimately depend on human decisions - at times risk-averse, other times bold. Leaders face constant forks in the road between comforting known paths and mysterious new ones holding potential. Progress follows the courageous who see beyond limits of the immediate and possible. And lifting others from doubt into confidence marks influence above all.

So how will you lead differently starting today?

Chapter Three

Influencing People

The nature of leadership has undergone a seismic shift in recent years. Whereas leaders previously exerted control through formal hierarchies and authority, the modern leader must navigate intricate networks of distributed power and influence. As organizations flatten and work is increasingly accomplished collaboratively across functions, firms, and even industries, having a title is no longer sufficient for impacting outcomes. Today's leaders must master influence – the skill of motivating others to follow without relying on command and control.

Those who cling to old assumptions about leadership do so at their peril. You cannot compel suppliers, partners, or even internal teams to work with you. Yet their participation is essential if you hope to introduce new initiatives, enter new markets, or drive organizational change. Skillful influencing is now mission-critical. As you expand your capacity to win over others, you gain the magic of leadership without authority. This allows your power to stretch far beyond what your formal role prescribes.

The Leader's Inventory: Your Influence Toolkit

Mastering influence starts with self-awareness about your preferences. Most leaders gravitate towards certain influencing approaches based on their experiences and personality. Common tactics include:

Building Rapport Through Shared Interests: Rapport establishes comfort and familiarity. Identify mutual interests, backgrounds, or experiences to find an emotional foothold with others.

Understanding Motivations Through Active Listening: Influence requires insight into what drives others' priorities and behaviors. Ask probing questions and intently focus on their responses to uncover their goals, fears, and perceptions. Allow them to share freely about themselves without interruption. You will gain invaluable context for aligning your agendas.

Offering Praise and Validation Generously: Few tire of being told they have talent, judgment, or integrity. Sincere compliments build goodwill and signal that you hold them in high esteem. As they come to value your opinion, your powers of persuasion expand.

Advocating Incrementally for Small Commitments: Big demands trigger resistance. Start by securing agreement on minor requests that allow for minor risks. Successive small wins build the confidence and appetite for bolder partnerships over time.

Modeling Trustworthiness Through Reliability

Influence flows from credibility earned over time. Make commitments carefully since nothing undermines authority faster than unfulfilled promises. Deliver consistently to validate others' belief in you. Their willingness to engage will track closely with their faith in your dependability.

While certain influencing styles come more naturally, an overreliance on one's comfort zone limits options. Become fluent in multiple approaches. Analyze each situation to discern the best fit for the players, dynamics, and objectives at hand. With experience, you will unlock new possibilities for exerting positive influence in virtually any scenario you encounter.

The Foundation of Teamwork

Organizational success hinges on teams that collaborate seamlessly despite physical distance between members. Achieving this alignment requires a shared emotional bond and confidence among colleagues. Rapport denotes feelings of harmony and mutual understanding. Trust means relying on others' integrity. Cultivating these connections empowers groups to operate at peak efficiency even when working remotely. Leaders play a vital role in establishing rapport and trust across distributed teams.

The Vulnerability Advantage

Interacting through screens dulls our instincts for developing alignments with colleagues. However, leaders can spark meaningful relationships by letting their guard down judiciously. Occasional transparency regarding mistakes, uncertainties, and differences can foster comfort and affinity within groups. Rather than feigning omniscience, acknowledge knowledge gaps honestly when navigating unclear situations. Ask sincere questions to elicit new perspectives and additional data. Frame disagreements in a constructive, non-confrontational manner focused on achieving collective progress. Invite critiques by implementing 360-degree feedback mechanisms through which all team members evaluate each other and leadership regularly. Follow-up discussions that openly explore diverse views signal receptiveness to input and change. Over time, candid yet compassionate exchanges lay the groundwork for mutual understanding and vulnerability-based trust.

Belonging Through Collaboration

Organizational success depends on a web of strong connections binding team members together, even when separated geographically. Technology facilitates communication but cannot replicate the richness of in-person engagement. Thankfully, leaders can nurture meaningful relationships virtually through genuine interest, clear communication, and celebratory moments. Investing in each dimension deepens interpersonal bonds for smoother collaboration across locations.

Seeing Team Members As Whole People

To become attuned to someone, shift focus beyond tasks and job titles towards a fuller appreciation of them as multidimensional individuals. Initiate conversations that uncover their personal passions, challenges, and aspirations beyond work. Customize interactions based on what energizes them rather than generic scripts. An introvert may prefer quick check-ins by chat while extroverts welcome lengthier video conversations. Note these cues and adapt accordingly.

Listen fully when members share, resisting the urge to interject your own experiences. Reflect back what you hear without judgingtheir perspectives to show comprehension. Express empathy and encouragement using words like "I appreciate you confiding in me about this difficult situation. I imagine anyone would feel disappointed, and I want to support you." Recommend reasonable accommodations if they face temporary hardship. Your willingness to meet people where they are builds trust in your compassion.

Likewise, recognize contributions often overlooked by formal reward systems. Catch members "doing things right" through specific praise, both publicly and privately. Thank those who volunteered assistance so they feel valued beyond department silos. Appreciation energizes elevated commitment to group priorities. Employees who feel respected as complete, complex people give their best in return through strengthened loyalty.

The Communication Feedback Loop

Fluid communication fortifies relationships, especially when collaborating remotely. Set expectations upfront about response times so members understand normal delays. Then follow through reliably. When situations demand your full focus, provide courtesy notifications to prevent perceptions of indifference.

Invite regular input through quick pulse checks like: "On a scale of 1 to 10, how clear are our current priorities?" Feedback exposes otherwise invisible barriers before frustrations escalate. Pose clarifying questions non-defensively to pinpoint improvement areas, then summarize what you heard: "So it sounds like our timelines feel vague and inconsistent. I appreciate you bringing this to my attention." Share resulting changes to reinforce that all voices hold value.

Just as critically, update proactively on team progress, wins and losses. Transparency regarding setbacks allows members to pitch in, echoing the mindset "We're all in this together." Frame challenges in the constructive light of collective growth rather than assigning blame. Celebrate milestones virtually through messages or video chats reinforcing forward momentum. Ongoing communication nourishes bonds of familiarity and comradery that propel teams through adversity.

Moments of Levity

Finally, counterflex the stresses of work with shared moments of humor and camaraderie. Recharge through informal virtual coffee breaks or trivia. Organize uplifting ceremonies for promotions, birthdays or anniversaries. Launch group challenges inviting friendly competition - who can compile the wackiest pet photos or best lockdown cooking fails? Build playlists with songs reflecting team members' moods and eclectic tastes. Moments inducing collective laughter release tension while etching fond memories that humanize interactions.

Positivity extends through everyday conversations as well.

- Greet members with warmth; express sincere optimism regarding capabilities.

- Graciously acknowledge different views during debates.

- Discuss challenges frankly but with assurance of prevailing together.

Consistent goodwill attracts reciprocal regard from your team members and other colleagues, this strengthening bonds to withstand inevitable disagreements. By brightening spirits and outlooks, leaders enliven teams for the long haul.

The connective tissue linking distributed groups requires proactive nurturing across multiple dimensions day-to-day. Giving full attention signals members' worth; inviting input builds trust; celebrating together fuels community. Leaders devoted to developing robust rapports prime teams for fluid collaboration despite distance - the lifeblood of organizational success in volatile times.

Empathy is the Heart of Leadership

Organizational success increasingly depends on navigating complexity and change with agility. This volatile landscape demands a reevaluation of traditional management assumptions to empower leaders who can guide teams through turbulence. Technical expertise no longer suffices; neither does an exclusive focus on bottom lines nor hierarchical control. The modern context calls for leaders adept at forging meaningful human connections even virtually. Empathy provides the gateway. By cultivating emotional attunement, leaders prime workplaces for resilience and innovation.

Seeing Signs of Struggle

Attuned leaders stay alert for subtle cues signaling that colleagues are struggling before small issues escalate into serious crises. Watch for rising absenteeism and missed deadlines indicating overwhelmed schedules. Note terse responses or withdrawn behavior departing from someone's usual sociability. Probe sensitively to uncover root issues rather than criticizing lagging productivity: "You seem really bogged down lately. What can I do to help you feel supported right now?" Simply voicing concern relieves pressure and isolation for those depleted.

Particularly as remote or hybrid arrangements blur work-life boundaries, monitor energy levels and engagement during meetings. Gather regular feedback to gauge people's stress levels anonymously if needed. Reach out to providerespite when you spot fatigue threatening their well-being and performance. Share relatable stories of your own ups and downs to reinforce that temporary troubles need not permanently affect one's prospects when met with understanding. Your willingness to meet people where they are, with judgment suspended, builds trust and loyalty to carry them through challenges.

Connecting as Whole People

Beyond workload management, empathy requires connecting with colleagues as multifaceted humans rather than mere functions. Set the tone by sharing judiciously about your life outside work — an upcoming vacation, enthusiasm for a new hobby, a child's achievement that sparked pride. Those listening realize leaders also navigate personal demands alongside professional ones. Ask about others' interests and families. Customize conversations based on learning styles you observe, whether someone prefers quick check-ins or lengthier discussions. Introverts may want to chat during a walk rather than video calls. Tailor your communication formats to individuals for mutual comfort.

When members reveal difficulties, recognize their courage in confiding through words like: "Thank you for trusting me with this sensitive situation. I know this level of candor requires vulnerability. I'm here to listen without judgment and provide any support you need." Follow through consistently, checking on them during the days that follow. Your steadfast concern through their trial strengthens loyalty beyond transient transactions. With empathy established as the foundation, you build a wellspring of goodwill to smooth relationships when inevitable tensions emerge.

Celebrating Common Humanity

Empathy's reach extends across departments through unifying events and symbols kindling our shared humanity. Launch informal talent shows allowing colleagues to express creativity beyond job descriptions, surfacing unexpected commonalities. Feature cross-functional "dream teams" collaborating on passion projects spanning organizational silos. Spotlight unsung heroes making quiet contributions behind the scenes.

Facilitate camaraderie through daily rituals: virtual coffee breaks, pet photo contests, soundtrack sharing allowing glimpses into people's personalities. spaces encouraging authentic connection enable relationships to deepen. Send handwritten notes when members experience loss, sharing candid stories of times you relied on compassionate leaders during your own hardships. Moments of vulnerability unite us more profoundly than roles or rankings ever could.

By championing empathy organization-wide, leaders transform disconnected groups into inspired communities. Colleagues once treated like commodities become cherished humans. Work powered by shared meaning and camaraderie gains momentum beyond incentives and orders. Employees at ease with being vulnerable themselves extend empathy spontaneously to customers, external partners, and new hires. Ripples of dignity and care diffuse outward, setting in motion exponential returns as recipients pay empathy forward.

The empathy advantage manifests itself through flexibility and innovation impossible under authoritarian regimes. People suggest unconventional ideas without fear of harsh criticism. They pivot collaboratively when conditions shift, not awaiting top-down instructions. Teams co-create solutions combining their complementary strengths because they know leaders will hear them out. Over time, empathy dissolves the hierarchies and siloes impeding organizations today, ushering in new possibilities.

An Ethic of Understanding

Practicing empathetic leadership simply means infusing compassion into all decisions and interactions. Seek first to understand colleagues' realities before assessing performance. Ask how you can support their goals rather than imposing yours unilaterally. Uphold consistent reliability so people know you will back them during turbulent times. Mentor emerging leaders to perpetuate these philosophies across your organization for sustainable culture change.

Leading with care for human potential unlocks discretionary effort and courageous innovation. Employees give their best in return through strengthened loyalty to each other and collective mission. By leveraging empathy's power, leaders future-proof their organizations to pursue purpose while upholding dignity across an intricately connected world.

Influencing Buy-In When You Lack Authority

Navigating organizational complexity often requires leading initiatives without formal oversight of key contributors. Securing budget, managing schedules, and coordinating teams grows exponentially harder when colleagues' cooperation stays voluntary. Prioritizing your project amidst competing demands depends on their goodwill. Yet exerting control contradicts your role. This misalignment risks chronic frustration.

The dilemma requires reimagining leadership as influence - the ability to motivate action without mandates. Certain techniques can help you rally and direct peers effectively even without authority. Incrementally, you gain supporters who choose participating, not due to obligations or carrots and sticks, but because they share your vision's purpose. Your informal sphere of inspiration expands. Savvy influencers transform solitary goals into collaborative victories through aligned interests and interpersonal bonds.

The Currency of Credibility

Influencing starts with building personal credibility so colleagues respect your vision and abilities even without a high-ranking title. Demonstrate deep expertise around the initiative's focal area through your contributions in meetings and projects. Ask thoughtful questions revealing keen strategic grasp. Share relevant articles and insights you uncover that offer value.

Later when pitching new ideas, reference previous successes, tying continuity between past and present ambitions. Remind peers of instances where your proposals or forecasts proved accurate. This track record lends weight when urging them towards subsequent endeavors.

You also influence by fulfilling all commitments made, whether large or small. Meet each deadline as promised. Follow through completely on key assignments. Come overprepared to working sessions. Establishing consistent reliability around deliverables prompts others to entrust you with greater responsibilities aligned to your goals. They believe in you because your actions earned their confidence over time.

Common Purpose Through Collaboration

Beyond personal accountability, influencers invest in understanding individuals' motives and goals. Ask questions to identify passions and pet projects. Look for shared interests to connect agendas. Illustrate how supporting your initiative advances outcomes they already care about. Draw explicit links between your vision and priorities held by critical departments or leaders.

Pose your request as an invitation to collaborate, not a demand for resources. "I cannot make this new product line successful without the expertise your team brings to optimization. This represents a chance to tangibly improve customer satisfaction ratings, which I know is a priority for you this quarter. Let's talk about how we can build this together." Framing your agenda through shared wins builds enthusiasm for cooperation.

On that foundation, encourage peers to shape elements of the project. Ask: "In an ideal world, what metrics would you track to gauge results?" People support what they help create, so influencers allow others to customize pieces that touch their daily work. When you demonstrate willingness to meld approaches, you seed ownership that motivates ongoing participation beyond initial agreement.

Relationships as Sources of Strength

While tactics facilitate buy-in, lasting influence flows from relationships. Show personal interest in those you seek to enroll. What workplace challenges do they find fulfilling? Ask about their kids, hobbies, favorite sports teams. Emotional connection kindles their desire to help you.

Likewise, when collaborating, affirm colleagues' contributions often. Recognize those who assist teammates despite competing demands on their schedule. Public messages to your allies highlighting their talents inspire engagement while earning their continued backing. "Alicia's creativity around reimagining supply chains is why our launch is trending so smoothly this quarter. Her Outside-the-box ideas represent exactly the culture our organization needs." Praise amplifies goodwill and momentum.

Even friction gets resolved more smoothly through strong ties. Address disagreements candidly but respectfully, emphasizing shared good intentions. Then reconnect on common ground. "I appreciate you challenging my assumptions. You raise important considerations. Our alignment around employees' best interests will make this an even stronger initiative." Keeping relationships intact enables progress through differences.

By aligning interests, empowering others, and deepening connections, you influence outcomes far exceeding your formal authority. Colleagues champion innovations they see as advancing collective values through your partnership. Over time, earned credibility and trust become sources of power no title can rival.

Key Takeaways and Final Thoughts on Influencing People

Key Takeaways:

- Influencing others starts with building personal credibility through expertise, accountability, and reliability. This earns colleagues' trust in your capabilities.

- Frame projects as invitations to collaborate around shared goals. Encourage customization to seed ownership and willingness to participate.

- Invest in emotional connections with colleagues through interest in their lives and consistent recognition of their talents and contributions.

- Monitor for signs of struggle in others proactively. Lend empathetic support early before small issues escalate into crises.

- Uphold compassion as an organizational philosophy by seeking to understand people's realities before assessing performance.

- Achieve greater buy-in by aligning interests with peers. Allow them to shape elements touching their work to promote engagement.

The Power of Influencing Through Partnership

Leadership in turbulent times hinges on galvanizing collective action towards what first seems improbable. Realizing ambitious visions against the inertia of established mindsets demands more than hierarchical control or incentives. Sustainably motivating people's highest discretionary effort requires influence - the capacity to inspire others' willing partnership in chasing dreams. By earning credibility, enabling ownership, forging connections, and leading with care, savvy influencers transform solitary goals into collaborative victories.

World-changing ideas never shift paradigms through lone genius but rather leadership that sparks aligned commitment across diverse contributors. The influencer's journey starts with earning peers' trust through accountability, reliability and results. This record lends weight when urging stakeholders towards new initiatives. However, tactical reliability only provides a platform. The capacity to enroll allies emotionally matters more. People support what they help create and care about. Influencers allow customization that speaks to colleagues' inner motives and goals. Shared vision propels cooperation beyond transactional gains.

Still, policies and projects fail to ignite absent human relationships undergirding the work. Leaders attending to struggles before people reach breaking points model that progress never necessitates harm. Colleagues give their best when assured of compassion should they stumble. With foundations of security established, teams turn vulnerabilities into catalysts for innovation, not reasons for fear. People uplift ideas because they know leaders will hear them out.

The influencer's role means living one's values visibly and elevating contrarian voices to forge breakthroughs. It is no easy path but rich with reward for those seeking to change the world. With partnership as the model, who will you invite on your next endeavor?

Chapter Four

Influencing Decisions

While managers possess formal authority over their direct reports, much of an organization's operations and decisions extend beyond any single leader's span of control. Convincing peers across divisions, senior executives setting overarching strategy, and external stakeholders to align with proposed initiatives often proves essential for ambitious leaders to drive impact.

Yet directing alignment cannot simply occur by fiat decree as with subordinates. Cross-organizational influence relies more upon persuasion, negotiation, and willing buy-in than command authority. Research on group dynamics provides valuable insights for leaders aiming to effectively shape collective decisions and actions rather than isolated gains within narrow domains.

First, gain stakeholder investment by broadening participation early in planning. Collaboratively formulating proposals alongside diverse contributors makes crafted solutions more resilient with sustained buy-in downstream versus receiving rubber-stamped sign-offs reactively. Bringing multiple lenses and mental models together from the start cements organizational commitments over the long-term by empowering broader shared ownership rather than lone stewardship. Leaders should facilitate these collaborative expansions proactively when conceptualizing ideas instead of risking notions being shot down for lack of co-creation during reviews.

Additionally, research shows overt displays of considering alternative perspectives builds credibility critical for influence. Leaders seen earnestly grappling with diverse inputs rather than rigidly adhering to preformed conclusions gain others' trust and inspire team cohesion. Facilitating open sharing around what objections or uncertainties remain before determining next steps proves more organizationally productive than declaring directives unilaterally. Promoting this behavior helps normalize a culture comfortable sitting with ambiguity, enabling the time and patience essential for complex coordination across company divisions with unique priorities and contributions.

Furthermore, leaders aiming to guide organizations opportunistically expand beyond internal perspectives alone. Seeking external insights from those in similar roles and industries sharpens contextual acuity and brings fresh angles otherwise unseen. Such networks should be fostered constistently, not solely when urgently needed, as genuine connections requiring vulnerability and reciprocity strengthen gradually through ongoing nurturing. Silos limit perspective; leaders must branch out across peer communities to multiply learning.

The Art of Influence

Daniel Kahneman, the Nobel Prize-winning psychologist and economist, extensively studied the psychology behind what makes arguments compelling and messages persuasive. His work sheds light on human decision-making biases and how to ethically leverage these insights to increase one's influence.

This section summarizes key research-based principles from Kahneman and other experts on the science of persuasion. It also provides practical guidance for leaders on employing these techniques skillfully and responsibly to convert ideas into actions.

Mastering the art of influence empowers leaders to shape critical decisions around budgets, staffing, priorities, and more to deliver results for the organization.

Anchoring for Framing and Reframing Debates

The first step to influencing any decision is determining how the issue will be framed in the first place. Kahneman's research revealed humans' tendency to make judgments by relying too heavily on the first piece of information offered when making decisions, called "anchoring."

Leaders can leverage anchoring to reframe issues in their favor from the starting point of debates by proactively suggesting a vision or parameters rather than re-acting to another's framing. Like a strong chess opening move that sets the tone for the rest of the game, how one anchors an issue influences people's perception moving forward by creating an arbitrary starting point that decision-making gravitates towards, even if irrational.

For example, if next year's budget is framed as needing to account for rising inflation and economic uncertainties from the outset, justifying any increase will be difficult. However, anchoring the debate by presenting opportunities for innovation, business growth, and revenue increases spins the dialogue positively towards investment from the beginning.

Anchoring effectively allows leaders to pave the way linguistically for decisions they wish to drive. Rather than surrendering influence by allowing others to control the narrative, savvy leaders anchor major issues on their own vision and terms.

Harnessing the Power of Social Proof

The similar human tendency to look to what others do for behavior cues, known as social proof, also plays strongly into influencing decisions. Kahneman demonstrated people depend on the signals, actions, and endorsements of others to guide what they view as correct more than objective facts. Leaders can harness this reflex by lining up credible supports to demonstrate momentum and validity behind ideas.

Secure respected senior executive sponsors who will lend their credibility and networks to endorse key initiatives. Kaiser Associates CEO George Walsh calls these influencer allies "powerful friends." Well-chosen influential supporters signal safety and strength to decision-makers who will likely follow suit. Their voicing assurance makes fence-sitters more comfortable saying yes. Additionally, their spheres of influence help expand backing organically.

Leaders must cultivate networks across, up and down to have endorsers in their corner when mobilizing for major initiatives. Identify power players and develop relationships before initiatives arise. Earning support from those considered leaders in their domain pays dividends when social proof is needed to swing decisions.

The Consistency Principle: Repeat Messages to Increase Belief

The next lesson from Kahneman's work that leaders can activate is leveraging the consistency principle - people's tendency to believe something is correct if they hear it enough. Familiarity breeds belief due to fluency bias. Messages repeated frequently seem easier to process and become embedded wisdom whether grounded in facts or not.

Leaders must steadfastly reinforce effective messaging to popularize ideas and make their narrative unavoidable. Khaneman advises trench warfare with arguments - keep hammering relentlessly. Avoid rushing or caving to pressure towards quick decisions during campaigns. Consistently broadcasting core tenets using similar language, analogies and expressions until widespread adoption follows.

Amazon CEO Jeff Bezos banned PowerPoint decks in executive meetings to reinforce this principle, requiring leaders to articulate ideas conversationsally through repetition. The ensuing familiarity increased buy-in far more than slidestacked pitches. Consistent verbal reinforcement cements messages for influencers until belief forms through continual exposure.

Leverage Emotion and Relevance

Kahneman also demonstrated humans rarely make decisions purely through facts and data. Decision-making involves emotional intuition more than rational processes. People believe ideas that tangibly resonate rather than cerebral arguments no matter how logically constructed. Leaders must ground influential messaging into the experiential to spark motivation. Demonstrate clear connections between ideas and what colleagues care about.

Statistics demonstrating rising customer dissatisfaction may receive head nods but fail igniting action without subjective context. However, leaders directly sharing impassioned customer grievances makes the issue hit home on an emotional level. Kahneman advises using killer factoids, anecdotes, case studies and any qualitative inputs that add vibrant color to rational data. Helping colleagues feel ideas through emotional relevance builds bonds and belief essential for influence.

Present Binary Choices to Progress Decisions

Another technique to progress influence is structuring decisions as binary choices, articulating an obvious preferable option rather than open-ended questions with many paths forward. Kahneman's research on choice overload showed offering limited options between a clear superior and inferior route forward avoids analysis paralysis that derails momentum.

Rather than broadly seeking input with non-specific questions like "How should we improve customer retention next quarter?" leaders can break down issues into explicit forks in the road. "Do we proactively assign customers account managers or rely on self-service databases to answer their queries?" Binary choices remove diffusion across endless options that breed inaction. Channeling decisions to efficient yes or no answers continues progression.

While occasionally necessary, leaving issues completely open-ended often spirals valuable meetings into vague theoretical discussions rather than driving towards concrete decisions. Savvy leaders frame issues as A or B choices between a constructive path forward versus unproductive status quo. The simplicity unlocks progress.

Leveraging Loss Aversion and Risk

Kahneman further demonstrated humans' general aversion to risk and potential losses typically outweighs the desire for equivalent gains when making decisions. Fears related to sinking time and resources into losing ideas holds many back more than hopes of upside. Leaders can activate this reflex to characterize any change as reducing threats rather than increasing uncertain growth prospects. CEOs obtain funding for innovative projects by presenting costs of legacy system failures rather than upside of unproven models. Securing safe passage often requires positioning ideas as securing stability rather than incurring risk.

Leaders can also ease colleagues past risk aversion through incremental buy-in escalation, Kahneman's "foot in the door" technique. Smaller initial investment seeds further commitment down the line until full buy-in crystallizes through momentum effect. A leader could gain executive approval for an experimental marketing campaign after framing upfront costs as negligible compared to doing nothing. Once early positive results emerge, subsequent expansion funding encounters less resistance. Baby steps build towards giant leaps through gradually accumulated buy-in momentum.

Asking Forgiveness Rather Than Permission

Finally, entrepreneurial leaders comfortable with judicious risk-taking may employ Kahneman's recommended approach of seeking forgiveness rather than permission. Bold leaders reluctant to await consensus or face rejection may forge ahead assuming supporters will follow positive results rather than oppose expending political capital to explicitly stop initiatives.

Greenlighting pilots under discretionary spending allowances or directly engaging customers on operating levels can demonstrate efficacy of ideas before official sign-off. Presenting supporters with proof-of-concept success and early social proof facilitiates after-the-fact approval. Kahneman does caution leaders ensure reasonable probability of success before this high-risk technique. Otherwise, acting without permission can quickly derail one's influence and career. Still, daring leaders equipped to absorb failures recognize sometimes it proves easier to retroactively gain buy-in than prospectively win permission.

Mastering influence accelerates a leader's ability to shape critical decisions at every level of an organization and drive change. While formal authority has limits, persuasion and willing buy-in prove limitless - but only with skillful strategy and execution. Key lessons leaders should incorporate when aiming to influence up, across or down include:

- Anchor issues on your vision upfront before narratives spin against you

- Secure support from credible endorsers to activate social proof

- Consistently repeat effective messages until widespread belief takes hold

- Leverage emotional relevance, not just rational data to convince colleagues

- Frame issues as binary choices focused on advancing solutions

- Characterize risk as stemming from inaction rather than potential gains

- Seek small commitments first to build buy-in momentum

- Occasionally, act boldly and ask forgiveness rather than timidly seeking permission

Master influencers avoid passivity, drive issues on their terms and ethically compel outcomes through understanding decision-making psychology rather than hoping colleagues eventually assist their aspirations. Leadership is not only about overseeing those directly below you, but marshalling collective contribution from parties across the entire organization to propel progress.

Critical Thinking and Persuasive Argumentation for Influence

Achieving shared buy-in around ideas and motivating collective action relies on a leader's ability to skillfully inform, inspire and influence team members. Specifically, honing one's capacity for persuasive argumentation proves foundational.

Constructing logical, evidence-based cases and conveying them to win minds and hearts determines leadership success perhaps more than any other competency. Persuasion fuels progress. Yet influence cannot be demanded or extracted by decree. Earning willing belief and follower investment through reason and resonance remains imperative.

In this section we discuss the foundational principles and tactical essentials for leaders to master argumentation, persuasion and critical thinking as per the maxims of rhetorical philosophy. Internalizing the following precepts empowers elevating teams by aligning them to the righteous path through inspiration's irresistible force rather than coercion's unsustainable pressure.

Principle 1: Lead with Empathy, Authenticity and Clarity

Influencing colleagues towards embracing alien ideas begins with deep understanding of existing mental models. Leaders can only illuminate the way for others from a foundation of empathy – truly apprehending audience sentiment before expecting audiences to apprehend proposed changes.

This demands embracing vulnerability through inquire rather than pronounce; listen rather than dictate. Welcome others sharing doubts, concerns and dissent.

Allow space for objections and dissent to surface freely without repercussion, as forcing conformity breeds far more resistance than rapprochement.

Further earn relational capital by rooting arguments in authenticity, logic and transparency. Manipulation may temporarily sway opinion through emotional trickery but fact-based truths standing firmly on their own merit prove far stickier. Treat all with dignity through simple, jargon-free language respecting comprehension variances across backgrounds. Finally, minimize ambiguity by structuring arguments to crisply convey intentions before urging realignment.

Leaders earn attention through humility, patience and clarity as the basis for credible influence attempts.

Principle 2: Rally Around Shared Purpose with Logical Reasoning

Once establishing ethos through character and conduct, influential leaders ground arguments in sound logos through reasoning. This demands logically constructing cases with clear claims directly addressing others' interests rather than one's own. Outcome-based thinking focusing on collective goals takes precedent over positional stances.

Compelling leaders architect arguments resembling geometric proofs that unravel mutual objectives into sequential steps for attaining them. This translates vision into roadmaps ordained by rational order, not arbitrary preference. Each subsequent milestone reinforces connecting current reality to the better tomorrow intended for all, brick by rational brick.

Weaving people's personal hopes into the logical sequence strengthens engagement emotional gravity. Voice how aligning with well-structured suggestions benefits not just business aims but also listener quality of life. Reason and relevance in tandem activate cognitive and emotional receptiveness, priming groups for pack migration towards progress.

Principle 3: Substantiate with Facts and Vivid Examples

The most convincing leaders buttress arguments with substantive facts from credible sources, balancing hard data with resonant illustrations. Statistics demonstrate logical proof points while case studies forge emotional connections between heads and hearts.

Bombarding audiences with abstract figures and scientific studies hamstrings influence due to information overload. Savvy leaders instead distill data into digestible insights explained through a few killer factoids and vignettes. These concrete examples embroider logical cases with sensory details breeding familiarity and retention similar to parables imparting moral lessons. Simple but vivid stores tap relatable experiences that linger sticky in memories to continually reaffirm judgment calls.

Principle 4: Acknowledge Alternative Angles

Leaders build both trust and critical thinking capacity by addressing rather than ignoring opposing perspectives. Demonstrating consideration of multiple angles conveys open-mindedness and underscores willingness to align with truth over ego. Teach audiences to expect and respect dissent within teams.

Rather than reacting defensively when views conflict with personal stances, influential leadersaine conflict. Creating space for pushback signals confidence while drawing out complete pictures for sound assessments. Even directly rebutting counterclaims combatively often proves counterproductive, as audiences interpret impatient responses as masking shaky foundations.

Instead, leaders poised to persuade reframe dissent through an impartial lens. First applaud surface issues, objections and uncertainties raised as vital to rounding out awareness. Yet persist spotlighting benefits of presented paths with gentler facts and sentiment. Seek shared understanding of all considerations, enabling groups to ultimately self-select optimal paths. People believe best what they convince themselves as personally truthful rather than force-fed.

Principle 5: Check Egos, Embrace Iteration

Finally, after constructing cases, engaging pushback and attempting influence, surrender attachment to outcomes remaining fixed. Audiences variably interpret identical information through their unique lenses. Rather than debating who holds superior wisdom, expect ongoing iterations towards improvement after initial suggestions.

Ego drives arguments aiming to establish what is right rather than optimize what creates mutually agreeable progress. Yet no single static truth eternally reigns - only collective advancement towards increasingly improved states proves sustainable. Leaders therefore plan persuasion campaigns on horizons of years, not quarters. Recognize perfect solution fallacy and instead value good faith progress however gradual.

Detaching proves instrumental in leadership influence. If building autonomous mastery and ownership around ideas for audiences fuels the primary purpose, zealous adherence to original formulations fails serving. Let go of means to focus on the ends and judge only against metrics indicating advancement towards North Stars. The rest simply provides indicators suggesting appropriate iterations to better arrive collectively.

By mastering empathy, reason and responsiveness, modern leaders unlock their highest potential to positively influence teams, organizations and societies. Progress depends directly upon the quality of persuasive argumentation skill directing change. An investment in elevating these capacities consequently fuels tremendous dividends towards the greater good through rippling positive impacts. And honing himself or herself the instrument towards these ends offers each leader the roadmap to transcendence.

This treatise presented core principles and tactical essentials for optimizing teams and organizations through high impact influence founded upon persuasive argumentation and critical thinking. By leading with empathy, grounding cases in logic, substantiating with facts and examples, encouraging scrutiny of alternatives and focusing on collective advancement over ego attachment, leaders masterfully earn buy-in around ideas that elevates all to greater potential.

Navigating Governance Frameworks for Influence

Identical proposals can result in wildly divergent outcomes depending solely on the decision frameworks employed, irrespective of merits or preferences. Understanding this reality proves foundational for negotiators seeking to drive favorable results by skillfully navigating varied rules of organizational decision architecture.

Organizational governance structures utilize a range of specific decision protocols, however several framework archetypes recur frequently across contexts. Broadly, these include unanimity rules requiring full consensus, majority structures tallying votes, designation rules privileging certain parties over others, and hybrid models blending aspects of these approaches.

In majority systems, option preferences of larger factions triumph over fewer supporters. Unanimity rules conversely compel reconciling all member concerns before ratifying choices. Designated decider protocols concentrate influence in specific individuals like chairs or executives empowered as primary determiners.

Familiarity with when organizations deploy pure models versus hybrid versions informs negotiator strategy. United Nations Security Council dynamics differ enormously from U.S. Supreme Court rulings or corporate annual meetings. Yet mastery of decision rules universally sharpens influence efforts through aligning tactics suiting operative constraints.

Majority Rule

Navigating majority-rule decision-making requires nuanced leadership to align differing interests towards shared progress. This article examines real-world case studies and evidence-based tactics for cultivating cooperative consensus among diverse stakeholders.

Mapping Interests and Fortifying Alignments: The first step entails discerning each member's priorities and intensities, as individuals rather than monoliths. Concentrating outreach on existing alignments fortifies your base coalition. Communication maintains ties pivotal on voting day. Influence hinges less on loudest voices versus attentive consideration across constituencies.

Cultivating "Fence-Sitters" and Expansive Issues: Strategically target less partisan members amenable to persuasion, starting from those impacting similarly pliable peers. Research shows creatively linking discussions to additional concerns creates opportunities leveraging negotiation techniques. Considering adjacent issues expands the range of reciprocal appeals addressing others' multifaceted priorities.

Tailoring Narratives for Target Audiences: Crafting tailored rationales harnessing distinct viewpoints strengthens resonance according to communication expertise. The ExxonMobil example highlighted an economic rather than ideological case to persuade the second largest shareholder. Supreme Court Justice Roberts asserting healthcare constitutionality through novel tax interpretation created space aligning an uncommon ally. Focusing communication according to unique constituencies builds durable coalitions.

Leaders adept at cultivating coalitions through understanding diverse interests and tailored persuasive narratives achieve broader consensus on complex issues. Addressing multifaceted priorities cooperatively builds sustainable progress. Organizations benefit from leaders uniting stakeholders towards shared purpose through respectful, strategic consensus-building.

Chair Decides

While certain roles concentrate authority, genuine influence emerges through cooperative relationships according to research. This article examines effective strategies for aligning diverse interests with solitary decision-makers through respectful stakeholder engagement.

Discerning Decision-Maker Priorities: Guiding proposals necessitates comprehending motivations driving priorities. Ideally, open-ended queries with leaders and confidants elucidate concerns to address strategically. When direct inquiries aren't plausible, past statements reveal perspective clues. Nuanced understanding grounds objective alignment.

Mapping Informal Networks: Few act independently; wise advocates identify informal advisory circles. For example, observing Meta's dynamic between Zuckerberg and Sandberg indicates their opinions' weight. Building access through respectful rapport with alternative routes influences outcome examination.

Addressing Multifaceted Stakeholders: While directly impacting leaders optimizes impact, colleagues observing could perceive impropriety versus team focus. Frame efforts garnering perspectives across constituencies to encourage cooperative atmosphere. Relational considerations sustain influence beyond immediate decisions.

Lasting influence emerges through cooperative relationships, not singular directives. Strategic engagement cultivates understanding serving diverse interests towards shared progress. Leaders adept at inclusive stakeholder consideration achieve sustainable consensus for optimized organizational outcomes.

Unanimity and Consensus

Achieving full agreement necessitates nuanced consideration of perspectives according to research. This report outlines respectful techniques for incorporating opposing views into cooperative solutions.

Active Listening and Understanding: Effective leaders make dissenters comfortable contributing according to experts. Publicly acknowledging concerns builds goodwill versus antagonism. Doctors addressing sale hesitations through tailored reassurances exemplifies proactive engagement.

Addressing Intransigence Respectfully: When persuasion fails, wise advocates avoid coercion, instead incentivizing cooperation. Raising obstruction costs diplomatically preserves relationships as neighbors sanctioned nations demonstrate. Alternatively, compromise through adjusted rules equitably incorporates priorities.

Tailoring Solutions to Diverse Priorities: Strategic cooperation identifies shared interests across viewpoints. For doctors, hospital partnerships complemented clinical passions through advisory roles. Augmenting junior compensation and honoring legacy inspired unanimous support. Incorporating unique concerns yielded collective priorities.

Lasting consensus emerges through respect and inclusion according consensus research. Addressing all perspectives cooperatively cultivates shared understanding and sustainable decisions. Organizational strength depends on leaders adept at incorporating diverse opinions through strategic, relationship-focused compromise. Nuanced consideration of priorities across stakeholders serves distributed progress.

Key Takeaways and Final Thoughts on Influencing Decisions

Key Takeaways:

- Influence proves essential for leadership as most decisions extend beyond a manager's formal authority. Skillfully persuasive argumentation provides a critical capacity for driving outcomes.

- Anchoring issues advantageously, leveraging social proof through endorsements, forcibly repeating messages, and framing decisions as binary choices can make arguments stickier.

- Empathy, logic, concrete evidence, addressing counter perspectives, and iterative improvement form the basis of highly influential critical thinking and persuasion.

- Navigating organizational decision frameworks offers another avenue to shape outcomes. Understanding governing rules better positions negotiators for success.

Unlocking Persuasion, Governance, and Progress Beyond Authority

Influence stands distinct from formal authority yet offers exponentially greater potential for leadership impact when wielded skillfully. While managers directly oversee employees, most initiatives rely on voluntary buy-in far across and above positional reach.

Cultivating capacities for empathy, reason and result towards securing willing investment unlocks otherwise impossible progress. Persuasion, not coercion, propels the visionary leader.

Specifically, astute influencers architect communication campaigns that strategically anchor dialogues, enact social proof through credible validators, repetitively reinforce narratives, and frame choices binarily to compel movement. They further ground arguments in care, logic and facts to relate to, while addressing doubts to preempt resistance.

Additionally, governance mastery multiplies outcomes for those negotiating key decisions. Few formal leaders singly determine high-stakes resolutions. But comprehending approval protocols and strategically addressing factional dynamics optimizes influence potential within constraint architectures.

Organization-wide accomplishments rely on coordinating dispersed contributors beyond limitations of individual might. Therefore progress-oriented leaders prioritize persuasion's force-multiplying skills towards rallying collective potential. Are we sufficiently strengthening inspiration muscles to progress goals demanding more than authority allows? The further the aim, the more this capability proves pivotal.

Chapter Five

The Power of "No"

Leadership comes with no shortage of demands and requests - from management, direct reports, colleagues, and clients alike. Learning to say "no" is essential to maintaining healthy boundaries that allow leaders to be discerning, set strategic priorities, and ultimately better serve their teams and organizations. However, declining asks or pushing back against the status quo may seem counterintuitive or even taboo in workplace cultures that value compliance and acquiescence. This article explores the nuances around exercising the power of "no" for improved leadership and influence.

On the surface level, leadership is perceived as having all the answers and being able to meet others' needs swiftly and sufficiently. However, more experienced leaders understand that demonstrating competence involves carefully considering what projects and tasks to take on based on bandwidth, resources, and alignment with broader goals. As executive coach Mike Myatt puts it, "Leadership is about how courageous you are and what you stand for." A key part of standing for something as a leader is proactively choosing what to say yes and no to, rather than reactively accepting every demand out of obligation or fear.

Reactions typically stem from habitual tendencies while responses reflect conscious choices made from a more objective, thoughtful place. Leaders aiming to shift towards greater discernment must learn to respond rather than react to requests and weigh the opportunity costs around agreeing to or declining particular projects. This empowers leaders to align activities to their team's highest priorities rather than becoming spread thin across disjointed initiatives that may not move the needle.

Of course, that is easier said than done when you have a demanding boss or collaborative culture that expects constant availability and acquiescence from leadership. Pushing back against the powers that be can seem like a career-limiting move. However, great leaders understand that agreeing to unreasonable expectations leads to unhealthy stress and prevents them from adding value in more strategic areas. The key is learning to decline certain asks in a polished, positive manner that clearly communicates your reasoning rather than blatantly refusing.

In practice, saying no with finesse takes forethought and preparation as leaders are often ambushed in the moment with asks they feel pressured to instantly accept or reject. While saying "no" or pushing back is rarely easy and often uncomfortable, it gets easier with practice. By preparing go-to responses and framing objections around protecting strategic priorities and team bandwidth, leaders can respectfully decline unreasonable asks. Saving "yes" for the right commitments empowers leaders to focus their finite time on moving the needle while preventing distraction and burnout. With discernment and courage, "no" ceases to be a dirty word and instead becomes a compass towards healthy, productive leadership.

Establishing Clear Boundaries for Effective Leadership

Leaders play a pivotal role in shaping workplace culture through the boundaries they set - both explicit guidelines and implicit allowances that dictate acceptable behaviors. This article explores how leaders can take ownership in constructing healthy, productive environments by clearly defining their own boundaries around what will and will not occur within their sphere of influence.

Defining Your Territory

Leaders occupy a unique position where they oversee their division or team's overall vision, personnel decisions, objectives, and norms. In many ways, they function as the "property owners" of their domain, with significant control in outlining expectations for those they manage - much like homeowners can determine what happens on their land. However, many leaders struggle to grasp the breadth of their boundary-setting authority or fear flexing that muscle. Understanding that, as leader, you govern your territory can be both empowering and daunting. You build and shape the culture through direct creation of rules and policies as well as indirect allowances of behaviors you permit to continue unchecked. Simply put - what you outline and what you allow combine to form your team's reality. Own it.

Drawing Healthy Lines

Once leaders grasp their position as culture architects, the hard work begins in discerning: What exact boundaries will foster a healthy, productive environment? Consider what conduct, contributions, and outcomes you aim to encourage versus discourage. Be precise about performance metrics, professionalism rules, and brand guidelines that align to your goals. Transparency and consistency are key in setting expectations. However, identify aspects of culture better shaped through allowance than rigid control. People thrive when given autonomy over how they collaborate and innovate within broad guardrails. Be judicious in micromanaging ad hoc processes. The most effective boundaries create clear lanes while allowing creativity and individuality to flourish.

The boundaries leaders construct and uphold have immense implications for team fulfillment and business results. What will you create or allow today to build a supportive yet successful workplace culture? The territory is yours to govern. Define it wisely.

Techniques for Saying 'No' While Preserving Relationships

Declining requests and pushing back against unrealistic expectations are essential leadership skills in today's fast-paced, demanding work environments. However, saying "no" understandably induces guilt and anxiety about offending others or being perceived as unsupportive. This article explores nuanced techniques for saying "no" at work with sensitivity and skill - maintaining healthy boundaries without burning bridges. By denying the request rather than the person, providing alternatives, delaying responses, and standing firm once decisions are made, leaders can preserve relationships and performance despite being unable to accommodate every ask placed upon them.

Separate the Person from the Request

Our initial inclination when asked to accept an unfavorable request is to reactively decline out of protection for our needs and limitations. However, it is critical we frame refusals around the infeasibility of the request itself rather than attacking the asker or their character. For example, rather than bluntly stating, "I can't take on any more work right now," try leading with empathy - "I wish circumstances allowed me to assist with this, but given my current bandwidth..." Such phrasing focuses on the logistical barriers to accepting while affirming mutual good intent.

Even if visibly frustrated, remain calm and professional in addressing why the request cannot be fulfilled at that time, whether due to other priorities, lack of resources, or mismatch with current goals. Convey there are understandable reasons for your decision by citing factual constraints. You are simply denying this particular ask, not expressing any judgment or ill-feelings towards the person themselves. Framing communications this way reduces defensiveness and preserves trust.

Suggest Alternatives

Cushioning a "no" by providing alternative solutions or compromises shows care for the asker's underlying needs despite being unable to meet the initial request. For example, if a colleague invites you to lead a new project when your plate is already full, rather than outright refusing with no additional context, propose, "I'm overwhelmed currently and unable to take the lead, but happy to consult in getting this initiative off the ground and identifying who on our team may have greater bandwidth."

Offering to connect them to other resources, take on a supporting role, or revisit the request at a later date with more availability demonstrates a spirit of collective problem solving. It signals that while this specific ask is infeasible now, you remain committed to the person and their professional success - preserving both the relationship and your boundaries.

Stand Firm Once Decided

The ability to firmly uphold choices once made also factors when learning to say no. If you acquiesce to pressure after initially refusing a request, it conditioning others to continually coerce you into overcommitment after being told "no." Leave no room for debate once communicating your decision by tying it directly to factual constraints - "Per my earlier points around my capacity being maxed out currently, I cannot take this on. How else can I help redirect this?"

If you do end up saying yes, fully own that commitment rather than rescinding later or taking on obligations reluctantly. Drop the internal tug-of-war, show up wholeheartedly, and refocus your mindset on accomplishing the task at hand with excellence given the present reality that you chose to accept.

Delay Deciding

The final technique that aids the art of refusal involves delaying your response if ambushed with a spur-of-the-moment request you feel unprepared to assess appropriately in the moment. Don't let the split-second pressure force you into an impulsive answer you later come to regret or reverse, which can cause whiplash on both ends. Instead, ask for reasonable time to consider the ask in light of your other responsibilities and availability: "Let me take a day to check my schedule and current bandwidth. I want to give this the thought it deserves rather than providing a rushed response."

Putting some space between the initial ask and your answer avoids reactionary decisions and allows you to evaluate any implications with fresh eyes before committing one way or another. More often than not, quick "no's" transform into measured "yesses" while impulsive "yesses" become regretful overextensions that you grow to resent over time. Delay allows wisdom and priorities to catch up with empathy and impulse.

Saying "no" with emotional awareness and tactical skill remains critical for leaders to maintain healthy performance and relationships amid competing priorities. By denying the request rather than the person, providing alternative solutions, firmly upholding choices once made, and giving adequate time to decide, leaders can preserve mutual understanding and respect while still enacting boundaries around overcommitment. Master the art of the gentle "no" - your team and your sanity will thank you.

The Art of Buying Time

As a leader, you will inevitably face a steady stream of asks and ideas from various stakeholders seeking your input, participation, or sign-off. While some align well with priorities and warrant support, others arise more spuriously and require deeper vetting and discussion before determining next steps. However, the instinctive temptation is often to provide an immediate answer of yes or no. This article offers techniques in the art of careful redirection - safely buying time rather than rushing to refusal or commitment.

By thoughtfully questioning ideas instead of dismissing them outright, you create space for constructive dialogue and avoid appearing reactive or close-minded. Similarly, delaying full endorsement opens the door to align demands to strategic goals versus chasing every whim. As we will explore, buying time enables both deeper relationship building and discernment around what initiatives warrant focus. Master redirection, and you master leadership agility amid complex decision making.

The Power of Open-Ended Inquiry

Let's first consider scenarios where others approach you seeking a quick answer on an idea or request. The instinct, especially for ambitious leaders eager to drive progress, is to provide rapid-fire responses. However, falling into this trap limits your ability to fully understand all facets of suggestions before you. Further, outright refusal without context risks appearing indifferent or self-interested.

Instead, leverage thoughtful inquiry as your first line of response when presented with new concepts. Rather than instantly approving or denying, reply by asking open-ended questions about goals, benefits, personnel needs, timelines, and connections to existing priorities. Not only does this allow you to gather helpful details, it also demonstrates engagement and care for team members' perspectives rather than coldly dismissing requests you feel less prepared to handle in the moment.

For example, if someone proposes taking on an additional project, instead of a knee-jerk "I don't have bandwidth right now," try responding with, "Interesting concept - help me understand more about the goals and payoff here so I can assess fit and priorities on my end." You smartly buy time for consideration while signaling you value their input enough to request more context.

In many cases, the very act of fielding your inquiries causes the requester themselves to identify potential flaws or realize certain constraints around their idea they had not previously considered. They essentially talk themselves into a more prudent direction without you having to play 'bad cop' shutting things down outright. Open-ended questions allow latitude for organic realization rather than cornering yourself into hardness. And even if asking questions fails to redirect the concept's trajectory, you gather useful details to make a more informed decision once additional time has passed.

Running Requests through a Coaching Model

Expanding on the theme of inquiry, you can employ a modified coaching model when ambushed with asks requiring swift commitment. Walk the requester through considerations similar to what an executive coach would reflect back to a client:

- Confirm the actual issue or goal this idea aims to address. Does a root cause actually exist versus chasing theoretical improvement? Has the need been well defined?

- Clarify who stands to benefit and why - what positive outcomes would manifest if implemented and for which stakeholders? What issues arise if not addressed?

- Understand existing constraints around resources, budget, and personnel availability. Would taking this on require de-prioritizing other existing projects and goals?

- Explore what support systems and structures need assembling for success. Is executive sponsorship secured? Is your team positioned to take on incremental work in this timeframe?

- Determine how this concept aligns with current priorities and targets at both team and organization levels. Does this accelerate progress or distract focus?

As you raise thoughtful points along each of dimensions above, several possibilities emerge. The requester may realize their idea requires further development first before meriting decision making given all considerations in play. Or by discussing fit with priorities, they see that other goals claim more immediate importance. Either way, by asking constructive questions, you thoughtfully redirect momentum rather than shutting concepts down or agreeing prematurely before properly understanding resource tradeoffs and strategic value.

And should the request still warrant serious consideration after this coaching process, you gathered critical data to make an informed call on next steps. Open-ended inquiry carries little downside risk while offering significant upside.

Wielding Priority, Process, and Personnel to Redirect

Unfortunately, not every situation resolves smoothly via mere conversation. Certain personalities championing requests aggressively resist redirection and seem dead set on securing your immediate endorsement. When facing stubborn persistence around a concept misaligned with goals or simply unrealistic given constraints, leverage priority, process, and personnel angles to prudently diffuse rather than confront directly.

For instance, looping back to examining strategic fit often gives the most straightforward path to pausing momentum. You can note, "I don't see how taking this particular approach accelerates the customer retention targets that are currently my team's chief priority based on leadership direction. Help me understand how you see this aligning with focusing our resources on the goals outlined last month in light of bandwidth considerations." Posing alignment to agreed priorities as a question refocuses attention versus outright disregard for ideas.

Likewise, if you sense the scope or expectation around a request gets defined unrealistically, play up the desire to set the initiative up for success by taking a process-oriented approach: "In concept I appreciate the value here, but see many interdependencies to consider first in order to de-risk execution before we formally commit. I suggest we take some time to map detailed dependencies, risks, and multi-departmental input required to get this right." Creating procedural stall tactics often contains over-eagerness.

Finally, don't hesitate to leverage personnel and sponsorship considerations if facing persistence around misaligned asks. Noting, "I don't believe we currently have the dedicated personnel required to achieve the outcome you have in mind given existing commitments. Perhaps we can explore whether [senior leader X] sees this fitting within their immediate priorities for Q1 and can lend their vision to properly scoping resource needs." Even gently suggesting an idea lacks appropriate buy-in sometimes hesitates forward movement enough that said concept loses luster in favor on some other passing fancy before circling back to you.

The Power of Inertia

As a closing note, remember that outside formally declining requests, leaders retain the discretion to simply take no action - what I term wielding the power of inertia. Beyond temporarily redirecting concepts that come your way, understand that very few ideas materialize into reality without committed champions pushing progress forward at every step. Numerous initiatives arise then fizzle out as momentum dissipates and individuals shift attention to the next novel notion that gains intrigue.

Therefore, once you effectively defer, delegate, or raise key considerations on requests brought your way, keeping them from securing formal approval, recognize that the vast majority whither in the frenzied innovation cycles across most corporations. Let the volume of ever-changing priorities facing your organization work in your favor; formal dismissal proves unnecessary when many concepts ultimately defeat themselves by failing to spark action amid resource constraints . Mastering judicious inertia removes much friction from deciding which commitments warrant supporting. In many cases, the healthiest approach lies in simply buying time - attuning yourself to when delay itself deals the death knell to requests outside your priorities.

The art of careful inquiry stands among the most constructive yet overlooked pathways leaders can adopt when navigating demands in complex environments. Preserving relationships and organizational trust rests on avoiding quick dismissal of ideas while also preventing distraction via chasing every new inquiry. Develop fluency in asking thoughtful questions, surfacing key considerations, redirecting based on misfit with goals and resource realities. Allow such skillful redirection buying you time for informed decision making or letting conceptual inertia run its course handle the dirty work averting distraction rather than resorting to blunt refusal by default. Master this nuanced balancing act, and you master the agility exemplary leaders come to be known for.

Key Takeaways and Final Thoughts on The Power of "No"

Key Takeaways:

- Learning to say "no" with grace and skill is essential for leaders to maintain healthy boundaries and strategic focus amid competing demands

- Reframing refusal around denying unrealistic requests rather than attacking the person or idea itself preserves trust and relationships

- Delaying responses, suggesting alternatives, and upholding choices empowers leaders to redirect momentum rather than bluntly refusing

- Open-ended inquiry buys time and surfaces key considerations to enable informed commitment to ideas that align to goals and resources

The Subtle Art of Redirection

Leading in dynamic environments inundated with asks and ideas inevitably requires discernment around which initiatives warrant focus and support. While ambition and eagerness to drive progress tempts quick commitment or refusal when presented with new concepts, redirecting momentum through thoughtful inquiry and consideration better serves organizational alignment and collaborative relationships. This chapter explored the underappreciated art of carefully saying "no"—deferring or denying requests rather than instantly approving or bluntly dismissing.

We first examined the interpersonal awareness required to refuse asks with emotional intelligence in ways that separate the person from the request itself. Rather than conveying indifference or judgment towards ideas, leaders able to frame "no" around logistical constraints and strategic misfit preserve trust and goodwill even when unable to assist. Furthermore, offering alternatives, upholding choices once made, and delaying reactive responses all demonstrate the consultative spirit found in redirection versus brute refusal.

Secondly, we discussed how asking constructive questions allows leaders to redirect conversations in ways that encourage requesters themselves to surface potential flaws or constraints around proposals they put forward. This organic self-redirection driven by open-ended inquiry averts tension while again providing information to make wise commitments. Likewise, when facing persistence around misaligned ideas, priority, process, and personnel-based concerns give straightforward means for pausing momentum.

Finally, we explored the underleveraged power of inertia in allowing concepts to defeat themselves when their champions fail to spark action amid resource realities. With so many competing priorities, most ideas that leaders carefully defer through skillful redirection struggle to gain sustainable traction downstream. The volume of ever-changing demands in most organizations aids this passive diversion once leaders thoughtfully question initiatives brought their way.

Developing fluency in strategic and compassionate refusal techniques distinguishes exemplary leadership in hectic workplaces replete with requests competing for airtime.

Chapter Six

The Partnership Principle

Leadership dynamics within organizations have grown increasingly complex over the last few decades. Hierarchies that were once strictly enforced and respected have given way to flatter structures with greater flexibility. Professional staff tend to push back against strict control and demand more input and autonomy. Deference to authority has declined sharply across society. So how should modern leaders relate to direct reports as well as managers both above and below them on the organizational chart? The key is adopting a "partnership principle" that frames all relationships as collaborative partnerships between equals, regardless of title or position.

The old parent-child hierarchy must be replaced with an adult-to-adult paradigm. Rather than wield power and control like an authoritarian parent, wise leaders empower their teams and elicit ideas and expertise from every level. They focus on developing capabilities over exerting authority. This starts with fundamentally changing how we conceive of organizational roles and responsibilities. Job titles and reporting lines will always be a structural reality but they need not define how we actually interact day-to-day. Except during periodic events like performance reviews, promotions and compensation changes, leaders should communicate with peers, direct reports and their own managers as valued partners in a shared endeavor.

Making this shift requires deliberately rejecting a command-and-control mindset that feels instinctual to many long-time leaders. Business language often reinforces hierarchy through labels like "subordinates" that subtly imply superiors and underlings versus colleagues. Even the idea of "managing people" evokes parental control over children unable to direct themselves rather than jointly guiding a group of adults. Unlearning these mental models is difficult but essential. Rather than unilaterally telling teams what to do and how, innovative leaders today empower them to help shape priorities, approach challenges creatively and drive results collaboratively. This distribution of ownership and accountability has proven key to agility, innovation and high performance.

Transitioning to the partnership paradigm is understandably difficult for some traditional managers accustomed to directing operations autocratically without input from below. They often worry that not wielding tight control means shirking their responsibilities. However, the opposite is true. No leader can possibly have all the answers in today's fast-changing, hyper-competitive environment. The best outcomes arise when leaders tap into collective intelligence rather than restricting direction and strategy to the perspectives of a few executives. Fearing the loss of status from working collaboratively with former "subordinates" holds many leaders back as well. But displaying vulnerability and embracing humility are vital to building trust and unlocking others' talents. The world has changed. Yesterday's lionized hard-nosed bosses have given way to empowering servant leaders focused on nurturing team members' growth and removing roadblocks rather than issuing commands.

Critically, the partnership principle applies at every layer of the organization. Senior leaders should collaborate with and actively listen to managers reporting to them rather than hand down rigid mandates. Those managers must in turn partner with frontline staff to define real problems and co-create solutions. And even entry-level employees should frame interactions with peers as cooperative efforts wherein each colleague brings complementary strengths to advancing shared goals. Regardless of tenure or title, seeing every team member as an esteemed partner makes them feel valued, taps their unique contributions and unlocks exponential performance improvements as employees at all levels increase engagement.

No leader has all the answers. Organizations must leverage intelligence, talents and passion across their workforces to nimbly respond to new challenges. By adopting the partnership principle's ethos of equality and seeking input from all quarters, today's leaders can empower teams to extraordinary heights. Though the hierarchical org chart may still stand, mutually respectful peer interaction holds the key to unlocking every employee's full potential and pioneering solutions. The path to collective brilliance starts with every leader rejecting outdated parental power dynamics in favor of a new collaborative partnership paradigm.

How to Partner with Senior Leadership

Navigating interactions with senior executives poses unique challenges for less experienced employees aiming to expand their influence. It's easy to unintentionally undermine your own credibility if you fail to shift both mindset and behavior when engaging top leadership. However, with concerted effort and preparation, any ambitious up-and-comer can establish themselves as a strategic partner rather than merely a junior employee seeking an audience.

The key is to avoid stereotypically "junior" conduct that signals inexperience and triggers well-worn hierarchical scripts. Common missteps include dominating the dialogue, failing to read verbal and non-verbal cues, dressing inappropriately, visibly lacking confidence, and force-fitting prepared speeches focused selfishly on your agenda versus responding directly to the actual discussion flow and leaders' needs. Each of these undercuts trust in your capabilities and judgment.

Adopting the Strategic Advisor Mindset

Acting as a partner starts with the right mentality: recognizing your role in enabling the executive's goals rather than viewing the interaction as subordinate groveling before exalted corporate royalty. You offer vital insights they lack; you are there to contribute to a shared mission. With this framing, outward behavior shifts naturally. Poise, active listening, adaptability and clear communication of value become second nature.

The key inflection arises when mindset shifts from junior to strategic advisor. No longer is leadership some exalted monolithic entity before which you grovel. They are partners who rely on your distinct perspective to address threats and capitalize on opportunities they lack context to see alone. Your seat at the table ensures well-rounded decision-making versus cloistered group-think. This mentality catalyzes vastly different behavior in high-stakes meetings - the self-assurance, flexibility and vision to influence strategy versus rigidly pushing pre-defined tactics.

Preparing Like a Trusted Advisor

This presence stems first and foremost from thorough preparation. Being ready to improvise requires deeply understanding leaders' priorities and pressure points, anticipating likely questions and directions, and carefully considering how your unique expertise can address these. Having clarity on your objectives for the engagement and realistic options for achieving them is equally key should the dialogue veer from the predicted path. Meeting preparation is far more complex than scripting a presentation you fully dictate. It demands mental wargaming to map various scenarios, tailor responsive talking points to each, and define alternative strategies should your initial proposal fall flat or seem misaligned with executives' needs in the moment. Audiences vary; situations evolve. Savvy partners enter each high-stakes meeting ready to pivot.

Take time to meticulously map probable questions and directions while carefully considering how your expertise directly serves leaders' interests. Avoid self-centered proposals unlikely to gain traction. Identify multiple options to accomplish agreed goals amidst unpredictable responses. Embrace exchanges as dynamic partnerships rather than platform for pre-packaged soliloquies. The objective is exhibiting deep understanding of strategic priorities, not proving cleverness or chasing tangents.

Thoughtful preparation breeds confidence and focus. You feel empowered to steer conversations because potential twists and turns don't catch you off-guard. You can read the room, clarifying leaders' true underlying concerns. You can readily repackage recommendations to better resonate. This flexibility and command inspire executives' faith in your judgment. Once they trust your strategic thinking and ability to rapidly respond to emerging priorities, they increasingly elevate you from tactical implementer to key decision-maker shaping initiatives at their side.

Confidence, Poise and Executive Presence

Presence matters too of course. Thoughts may race internally, but outwardly you exhibit poise and polish: steady voice, direct eye contact, active listening. You dress professionally, epitomizing executive presence to signal your sophistication. In discussions, you balance concision, forcefully communicating complex concepts clearly while avoiding excessive wordiness that tries leaders' patience and focuses attention inward. Throughout, you maintain humble confidence rooted in expertise versus arrogance.

Alongside flexibility, executive presence matters immensely. Project steady poise through direct eye contact, active listening and concise, clear responses revealing sophisticated communication skills. Dress professionally, epitomizing leadership polish. Convey complex concepts conversationally, grasping nuance and context to persuade diverse stakeholders. Demonstrate humility by seeking to understand before being understood. This combination earns peers' respect and leaders' trust in your capabilities over time.

Building Strong Relationships

Finally, remember that strategic advisors build relationships before reputations. Establishing enduring influence requires consistently contributing novel solutions tied directly to business goals versus self-centered pet projects. This partner paradigm pays compounding dividends over time as executives increasingly default to leveraging your insights to inform major decisions, cementing your role as one of their most trusted counselors.

Eventually, cementing this "partner" role earns seats at tables where pivotal discussions happen well before decisions get made. But rushing to establish yourself overnight frequently backfires. Patience, consistency and reliability create crucial bonds and belief in your expertise that enable lasting influence.

Transitioning from junior staff member to strategic leader undoubtedly demands new mindsets and skillsets still being forged for up-and-coming talent. But by preparing thoroughly for high-visibility interactions, emphasizing value generation for company leaders over personal promotion, and conducting yourself with flexibility, polish and poise in the room, your influence elevates exponentially. Leaders notice and reward those exhibiting the air of strategic partners versus nominally subordinate individual contributors. Adopt this presence and thinking in all internal engagements and your days spent anxiously seeking audiences and approval shift to enjoying automatic seats at tables where key decisions happen.

How to Partner with Less Senior Colleagues

Within companies, there unfortunately persists an outdated model of leadership centered upon absolute authority and unquestioning obedience. Behaviors like lecturing subordinates without genuine listening, barking orders without explanation, interacting abrasively, and outright disregarding input signal a view of team members as inferior implementers rather than partners.

This imposed isolation, transparency about priorities and rationale, breeds frustration. It makes employees feel disrespected, incapable of contributing meaningfully, and incentivized mainly to avoid reprimand. Over time, talent disengages. Trust and loyalty erode. Alienation replaces ambition. Teams staffed with brilliant professionals default to merely adequate output. They fulfill assigned duties without exercising creative license to tackle challenges proactively because leadership relationships feel transactional rather than collaborative.

Benefits of a Partnership Paradigm

The contrasting approach - conceiving of a team as equal partners unified by shared goals - unlocks exponential mutual value. With a partner mindset, leaders recognize that each employee offers unique and essential expertise. They see role hierarchy as simply structural versus inherent superiority, emphasizing collaboration over control. Partners actively support and empower one another to maximize collective talent for breakthrough solutions.

This starts with listening first and speaking second. Ask thoughtful questions before providing every answer. Invest time broadening contextual understanding. Express genuine interest in team members' insights rather than feigning consideration while awaiting chances to dictate. Doing so builds psychological safety where people feel comfortable challenging assumptions. Curiosity spurs clearer communication of priorities and rationale behind decisions, further bolstering ownership and commitment.

Benefits for Leaders and Teams

Embracing partnership paradigm benefits flow both ways for leaders and team members. For staff, they gain greater understanding of how their work enables corporate strategy. Responsibility increases development opportunity. Autonomy fuels engagement through freedom to innovate and make local decisions without micromanagement. Purpose and potential both rise, realizing and retaining top talent more consistently.

Simultaneously, leaders gain richer visibility into daily operations. Morale, productivity and retention all tend to improve significantly. This misconception persists that distributing authority softens accountability. In reality, increasing ownership strengthens it. The highest performing teams self-motivate and self-govern based on common cause with minimal oversight needed. As vision and values synchronize bottom-up, leaders can shift focus to higher-order concerns.

Making Partner Leadership Stick

Transitioning to a shared leadership model rooted in mutual trust and accountability understandably disrupts some managers' comfort zones. However, ample evidence argues that collectivized vision outperforms edicts from the top on every metric. The first step is simply recognizing that no leader has monopoly on good ideas. Solutions bloom when all contribute.

To catalyze this culture shift, leaders must first role model desired behaviors. Take time to explain context around decisions and demonstrate receptivity to feedback. Spotlight contributions of team members who lack traditional visibility. Celebrate collective wins, however small initially. Adjust policies inhibiting collaboration or autonomy.

Instituting such changes sends an unequivocal signal: going forward, partnership practices will define leadership here. This lays cultural foundation for the high engagement, innovation and performance that only robust partnership can unlock.

Building and Sustaining Partnerships

Leadership authority ultimately stems not from titles but willingness of others to follow. No matter your nominal hierarchical rank, absent genuine reciprocal influence grounded in trust and support across an empowered team, any supposed "leader" merely postures. True leadership forms through negotiated partnership between leader and led. It relies inherently on earned authority, not ordained power.

The highest-performing leaders embrace a "partnership" ethos, forging ties rooted in mutual respect and reliance. Rather than dictating by fiat, they co-create direction collaboratively. They unlock others' talents by conveying confidence in teams' capabilities and intentionally distributing ownership. They exchange feedback openly to align on priorities. By investing in personal connections and modeling vulnerability, partnership leaders inspire loyalty and dedication that propels teams to extraordinary heights.

In contrast with authoritarian or transactional leadership models where followers mainly comply reactively due to carrots or sticks, the partnership paradigm engages individuals' intrinsic motivations. People give disproportionately more to leaders who genuinely care for their development and seek to marshal followers' full range of contributions rather than siloing staff in narrow functional roles. Partnership sets the stage for innovation by signaling all ideas deserve consideration on merits versus status.

The Performance Dividend

Extensive research confirms that partnership leadership creates exponentially better employee experiences. Across outcome metrics from strategic clarity to engagement, teams led collaboratively substantially outperform groups directed hierarchically on every dimension. For example, scientists have found that 89% of employees working under partnership-focused leaders feel optimistic regarding their organization's future trajectory. Contrast this to 81% for paternalistic leaders, 72% for transaction leaders, and a mere 48% for adversarial managers.

The data similarly reveals significantly higher engagement, satisfaction and performance among employees of leaders who treat their teams respectfully as partners versus those who rule unilaterally by diktat and dismissal of input. Fostering psychological safety where people feel valued partners in a shared endeavor rather than cogs in a wheel fundamentally shifts mindsets toward greater ambition and accountability.

Steps Toward Partnership

Transitioning leadership culture to embrace collaborative partnership admittedly disrupts established hierarchies. However, ample proof argues that decentralizing control this way boosts results across metrics. So how can managers adopt behaviors that nurture partnership dynamics with teams?

The first step entails honestly evaluating current practices using the frameworks discussed. Identify areas where you currently diminish others' contributions without intent by overlooking acts of leadership or failing to explain rationale. Consciously look for hidden innovators and unsung standouts rather than focusing narrowly on known stars.dcl

Next, set expectations by clearly communicating the importance of collaborative leadership for organizational success. Reinforce interdependence: framing work as "my team" not "my people." Celebrate team over individual accomplishments. Promote informal peer-to-peer collaboration. Demonstrate receptiveness to feedback and suggestions. Through modeling partnership yourself, its contagion will spread.

Partnering and Collaborating Across Functions

Imagine an organization where marketing, sales, product development, and other departments operate in silos, rarely interacting or aligning efforts. Communication flows poorly across internal boundaries. Insight stays trapped in functional stovepipes rather than informing organization-wide strategy. Leaders double down on narrow departmental metrics at the expense of the business's overall health.

Now envision an alternative reality – one where diverse experts across departments team up routinely to tackle projects. Sales and marketing co-create messaging grounded in a shared customer perspective. Product and engineering collaborate to build solutions tailored to user needs. Cross-functional committees jointly assess challenges and opportunities from multiple lenses. In this environment, insight and creativity flourish exponentially.

The latter scenario brings the myriad benefits of cross-functional collaboration to life. Cross-team collaboration occurs when employees from separate internal groups work together in any capacity towards common goals. It may entail informal information sharing, collective brainstorming, or structured processes for developing products and campaigns shoulder-to-shoulder.

Cross-functional collaboration offers no silver bullet. However, organizations that embrace it reap gains in communication, innovation, productivity, and alignment over those that allow departmental silos to calcify. Lean too heavily into structures that isolate expertise by function, and organizations become disjointed and schizophrenic. But connect diverse perspectives across internal boundaries, and they transform into cohesive, versatile entities capable of seeing around corners and pivoting on a dime.

Keys to Effective Cross-Functional Teams

Cross-functional collaboration delivers immense latent value. Yet realizing its full potential takes concerted effort. Early attempts frequently fall victim to the inertia of established hierarchies, metrics, and processes that incentivize insular departmental thinking over organization-wide cooperation.

Research suggests three-quarters of companies struggle getting cross-functional teams to perform well. Fortunately, the path to progress holds certain guideposts:

Identify Executive Sponsors: Gains ONLY happen through leadership emphasis on collaboration as a strategic priority. Loosely encouraging teams to coordinate without systems support breeds more confusion than cohesion. Executives must champion cooperation across functions in words AND deeds.

This means appointing leaders tasked with governing and facilitating cross-functional efforts. They design protocols clarifying expectations, moderate complex dynamics between teams, and create environments psychologically safe for joint work. Getting collaboration to stick requires structuring the leadership context around it.

Align on Common Goals: By definition, collaboration means working jointly towards shared aims. Yet functional silos often drift into orbit around disparate priorities that seem loosely if at all connected on the surface. Engineering obsesses over ship dates, while Sales fixates on deal targets. Absent broader alignment, they struggle seeing how cooperation furthers narrower pursuits.

Leaders must continually reinforce overarching visions and outcomes that bind the organization together. This provides a unified frame of reference as teams tackle problems jointly. Grounding collaboration in common goals gives efforts meaning and continuity. It allows cooperating groups to lock arms tighter in service of ambitions all have a stake in rather than operating as disjointed entities bobbing alongside one another.

Empower Teams with Ownership: Cross-functional cooperation flops without mindset shifts towards shared accountability. Too often, attempts feel forced – a mandate from above rather than opportunity for mutual gain. Leaders must cultivate understanding across teams about how working together actively enables departmental and individual success.

The most effective organizations adopt a "one company" mentality - a collective identity that supersedes functional identities. Politicking for resources yields to transparent priority setting. Information gets exchanged freely between groups. Subject matter experts work alongside colleagues to multiply insights' impact. People help across historic divides because all goals feel intertwined.

Nurture Relationship Networks: Formal structures alone cannot generate cross-functional collaboration. The social connections undergirding organizations more profoundly enable cooperative efforts. Think of it as leaders putting intentional glue between departments. This entails actively fostering interpersonal cohesion across teams via team building rituals, job rotations, lunch &

learns, cross-training in peer groups' expertise areas, and centralized platforms that make accessing counterparts frictionless.

Innovation emerges through serendipitous encounters between diverse thinkers. Nurturing relationship networks lays foundation for chance meetings where inspiration strikes. It breeds familiarity and trust between groups otherwise prone to eyeing those on "the other side" warily. Intentional community building forms the human conduits through which creativity flows organization-wide - the lifeblood of nimble, resilient, and ultimately dominant modern enterprises.

Tactics to Operationalize Cross-Functional Collaboration

With guiding principles established, what tangible steps can organizations take to bake cross-functional collaboration into everyday reality? Consider the following proven tactics for implementation:

Stand Up Cross-Functional Leadership Bodies: Formalize executive commitment to cooperation by creating specialized teams charged with nurturing it. These cross-functional committees or councils own setting vision, creating standards, and governing programs related to inter-departmental partnership.

They model behaviors – transparency with one another, checking narrow interests at the door, and commitment to organization-wide optimization vs functional gains when setting direction. Their unified support and oversight gives lower-level leaders cover to prioritize collaboration over traditional departmental goals.

Launch Shared Initiatives: Set up joint projects requiring coordination by design. For example, have personas or customer journey mapping done not by individual teams but collectively in workshops. Make integrated planning sessions the forum for defining priorities and strategies. Ensure product development, marketing, and support all have seats at the table when laying technology roadmaps.

Repeated shared experiences foster mutual understanding of how various groups create value differently. Over time, mental walls fall as teams feel invested together in driving outcomes. Participants export lessons learned back to departments as evangelists for cooperation's power.

Structure Workflows Around Information Sharing: Break down silos by re-architecting legacy workflows assuming isolation. Marketing and Sales should collaborate intimately at every client touchpoint when passing leads between teams. Feature feedback funneled directly from Support and Customer Success should feed Engineering and Product's planning.

Enable seamless exchange of knowledge across team boundaries. For instance, create centralized wikis or repositories with access to all. The more that insight informs decisions across the board, the tighter strategic alignment will grow.

Incentivize Cross-Functional Goals: Take cues from the OKR methodology by setting shared objectives and key results focused specifically on collaboration. This makes cooperating across historic divides a collective priority. Establish metrics that reinforce "one company" thinking – customer satisfaction and lifetime value instead of sales quotas or traffic targets assessed by each isolated domain.

Celebrate mutual achievements over individual or departmental ones. Ensure performance management frameworks include peer feedback and ratings from other groups. Every lever should send the message that multiplying success requires working across functions jointly.

Benefits of Effective Cross-Functional Partnership

Why undertake the hard work of nurturing cross-team collaboration in light of deeply etched legacy habits? In short, because organizations recognizing they face adapt-or-die business environments realize cooperation unlocks exponential value over go-it-alone approaches.

The case for collaboration stems from multiple angles. First, it enables superior customer insight to inform decisions companywide. Marketing, Sales, Support and Customer Success each hold unique but fragmented understandings of users. Synthesized holistically, truth emerges about motivations and pain points that no single perspective could ever reveal. With all teams taking an outside-in view grounded in shared empathy, solutions better solve for human needs.

Second, it accelerates innovation. Creativity and inspiration swell from collisions between different mental models. Engineers see possibilities beyond marketers' imagination, while designers envision elegance where finance staff default to spartan functionality. As leaders facilitate interdisciplinary collisions, fresh ideas with magnified impact emerge.

Additionally, communication dramatically improves both within central hubs and out to customers. Messages resonate louder when functions harmonize content and delivery for integrated amplification across channels. This consistency also fosters trust in customers, conveying coherence rather than disconnection internally.

Moreover, cooperation enables higher performance execution. More seamless handoffs between teams working interdependently on shared clients mean less friction impeding complex processes. Sales and Services seamlessly picking up threads from Account Management limits fumbled balls. With less repetition or redundancy from poor synchronization, people accomplish more collectively through tighter coordination.

Finally, cross-functional alignment naturally enhances culture for employees by breaking down perceived caste barriers between groups. Camaraderie blossoms when project teams blend staff from Finance, IT, Marketing. Recognition arises based on collaborative behaviors versus individual attainment. People bond over shared wins. Everyone feels seen as an equal contributor working towards common cause. Solving multidimensional problems requires multifunctional perspective and partnership. By proactively nurturing cross-team collaboration, today's leaders equip organizations to continually reinvent themselves - essential to sustained relevance and outperformance.

Key Takeaways and Final Thoughts on The Partnership Principle

Key Takeaways:

- Leaders must shift from command-and-control to a partnership paradigm that treats all employees as valued partners in a shared mission, empowering teams through trust and accountability.

- When engaging senior executives, prepare thoroughly to demonstrate strategic thinking, offer insights tailored to their goals, and convey confidence through flexibility, polish and vision.

- Lead less experienced employees by listening first, asking thoughtful questions, recognizing their expertise, and conveying respect for their contributions.

- Sustain partnerships by co-creating vision and strategy, facilitating shared experiences that foster mutual understanding, encouraging transparency and information sharing, and incentivizing collaborative behaviors.

- Enable seamless collaboration across functions by appointing executive sponsors, nurturing relationships between teams, architecting system workflows around cooperation, and setting shared cross-functional goals.

Achieving Organizational Excellence Through Partnership

Leadership boils down to galvanizing collective potential in pursuit of shared goals. But dated paradigms still prevail of employees as subordinates rather than partners, of wisdom flowing only top-down rather than emerging bottom-up. Rigid hierarchies and habits sabotage engagement. However, by embracing collaborative partnership at all levels, organizations can unlock ingenuity and outperform.

This chapter has explored frameworks for partnership across several crucial leadership dimensions. First, it examines how to engage your own managers more collaboratively by demonstrating strategic thought leadership versus seeking approval alone during executive interactions. Preparation establishes credibility as their peer and advisor rather than junior player.

Additionally, it discusses lifting less experienced individual contributors through humble inquiry into their unique expertise and empowering them to drive impact. Listening and recognizing contributions conveys their value and breeds loyalty to organization-wide advancement.

Beyond hierarchies, enabling collaboration across functions multiplies innovation via interdisciplinary collisions. Appointing cross-functional sponsors, architecting systems around sharing, and nurturing communities of practice brings down silo walls. With cooperation as the keystone of culture, organizations transform from fragmented to fused.

Of course, leadership remains an endless journey. But embracing partnership as the lifeblood of organization evolution sets in motion self-reinforcing cycles of participation and performance to take entities to soaring new heights. Can we lead partners rather than subordinates, collaborators rather than competitors internally? If so, no summit lies beyond reach.

Chapter Seven
Negotiations

Negotiations, at their core, represent opportunities for collaborative decision-making and mutual understanding between parties. However, they are often mischaracterized as adversarial battles where one side must prevail over the other. This combative approach typically fails to produce optimal outcomes for either party. As an alternative, positive negotiations offer a pathway to achieve win-win scenarios that satisfy the key interests of all involved.

Preparing for Successful Negotiations

Whether resolving internal conflicts or closing sales worth millions, negotiations permeate leadership. Done constructively, they empower shared victories through mutual understanding. Done poorly, negotiations forfeit progress through assumptions, misalignment and distrust. Surprisingly, even seasoned professionals neglect preparation which enables one to enter talks with clarity of purpose and possibility. The following explores foundational insights for unlocking negotiation success.

Seek Understanding Before Demands

Imagine entering complex negotiations lacking context behind counterparts' constraints, motivations and deal breakers. You now depend on guesswork rather than insight when assessing options. Any proposals herald from your reality alone, severely limiting potential fit. Such ignorance ensures laborious back-and-forth bargaining around what should smooth progression towards mutually beneficial terrain. Therefore, postpone overtures until after inquisitive assessment regarding the true landscape before you.

The most successful negotiators adopt a learner's mindset in early discussions, asking thoughtful questions that reveal underlying interests, pressures and priorities guiding those across the proverbial table. They focus on comprehending challenges first, brainstorming solutions second. Far too many unprepared negotiators become preoccupied with immediate proposals rather than foundational relationship building through purposeful listening and mutual understanding. Resist transactional tendencies. Progress depends on unity, not just compromise.

Understand Wider Perspectives

Negotiations often stall when parties adopt narrow, self-interested positions without acknowledging legitimate alternate views. Breakdowns escalate when demands seem insensitive to shared challenges complicating simplistic resolutions. Therefore, dig deeper into the systemic factors and pressures shaping your counterparts' stances.

What market, cultural or operational realities justify their hesitation? Who else behind the scenes influences their orientation? What would constitute a "win" from their vantage point? Again genuine curiosity and suspend preconceived judgments as you walk figurative miles in their shoes. Seek their authentic worldview.

Uncover Greater Possibility

Equipped with broader context regarding interests and constraints across the invisible negotiation table, creative solutions emerge you may have otherwise overlooked. Having paused reactive exchanges in favor of insight gathering, both parties now collaboratively introduce possibilities aligned with mutual success factors. Brainstorm options through an inclusive "us" lens rather than combative "yours vs mine" perspective.

Successful negotiating depends on this explorative space between initial education and formalizations where potential flourishes. Replace debate with expanded ideation that interweaves both parties' interests into joint decisions. Herein lies the art of insight. Greater ambition arises when negotiations elevate collective aspirations rather than divide limited resources. The whole outweighs the sum of its parts.

Wise negotiators understand preparations granting clarity into all pertinent stakeholders cultivate fertile ground for integrative agreements. Securing optimal outcomes requires addressing complex systems, cultural nuances and competing constituencies shaping the landscape. Do your homework, comprehensively mapping your ecosystem of influence. Progress does not arise by negotiating around the table alone but rather by unlocking possibility for those surrounding it as well. Your counterparts' success must factor into your own definitions. When negotiations focus on creating rather than claiming value, mutual victory persists ever possible.

The Win/Win Mindset

The essence of positive negotiation lies in the adoption of a win/win mindset oriented around mutual gains. This requires viewing negotiations not as tricks to fool or defeat the other party, but rather as collaborative efforts aligned towards shared interests and desired outcomes. Combative posturing or zero-sum positioning often triggers unhelpful fights that risk suboptimal resolutions. In contrast, a win/win approach recognizes that the greatest victories arise from mutual understanding rather than brute force.

This mindset understands that multiple parties can successfully get what they want from a single negotiation. It focuses on expanding the pie before dividing it up. For instance, in a salary negotiation, rather than viewing it as a pure dollar figure battle, both parties share underlying interests related to talent retention, new initiatives, career development, work-life balance and more. By broadening the scope of variables, more potential exists for mutual gains. One party may concede on immediate compensation but secure funding for sabbaticals and training to aid long-term career growth. Through open communication, both feel their core needs were addressed.

Interests Over Positions

Foundational to the win/win concept lies a focus on interests rather than positions. publicly stated demands often serve as positional posturing without revealing motivating interests. For instance, initial salary requirements represent opening positions that fail to communicate fundamental needs around career growth, work-life balance, job satisfaction and more. These interests prove far more insightful for discovering common ground.

As leaders, when negotiating we must guide parties away from positional battles towards interest-focused interactions. This requires asking thoughtful questions, actively listening, and seeking shared goals rather than arguing over explicit demands. By uncovering why the request or offer was made and what the underlying needs are, new variables and trade-offs emerge enabling expanded possibilities.

An interest-based approach also builds empathy and psychological safety for all involved, setting the stage for integrative agreements. With trust established, parties feel comfortable expressing even confidential interests that need accommodation. This transparency around personal, business and cultural needs magnifies potential win-win landing zones.

Positive negotiations require a collaborative win/win mindset focused on satisfying shared interests rather than competing over positions. This article provided an introduction to this transformational approach aligned with modern leadership environments that value transparency, communication and understanding. In competitive negotiations, everyone risks losing sight of collective goals amidst the positioning and posturing. In contrast, interest-focused interactions lead to integrative agreements and mutual victory.

The Negotiation Process

Negotiations often feel akin to navigating an intricate dance where missteps threaten to undermine positive outcomes. However, when undertaken collaboratively, they can engender mutually beneficial solutions. This requires parties to jointly chart a path aligned with shared interests rather than seeking to impose proprietary logic or demands. By progressing through key phases focused on education, creativity and preemptive problem-solving, negotiators build the foundation for integrative agreements. This article outlines these constructive steps to guide leaders towards negotiating with understanding.

Define the Common Opportunity

Before detailing solutions, negotiators must first align around the core challenge or opportunity catalyzing discussions. Rather than immediately advancing partisan proposals, take time to educate each other on current needs and circumstances prompting collaboration.

- What obstacles or roadblocks face each side that partnership might help navigate?

- Where could synergies or efficiencies manifest through cooperation?

- What capabilities or assets does each party offer that might empower and strengthen the other?

This foundational education phase paves the way for solution brainstorming by first ensuring all stand on common ground regarding impetuses. It also builds psychological safety and trust as parties demonstrate authentic listening and learning rather than combative dismissal of divergent positions. With core needs empathized and roadblocks understood, creative win-win proposals soon emerge.

Uncover Underlying Interests

With the scene set, address underlying interests informing negotiators' desires rather than explicit positions alone. For instance, initial salary demands often reflect an unspoken holistic need around career development and work-life balance.

Seek clarity around what key outcomes each party hopes to gain through collaboration.

- How do they define success?

- What limitations or constraints must any solution navigate?

- What flexibility or alternatives merit consideration?

This emphasis on interests over positions proves critical as parties now engage based on motivations not demands. Previously incompatible proposals often share interests allowing reimagined, mutually-acceptable options to emerge through ongoing dialogue and brainstorming. However, do not become preoccupied with immediate solutions yet - retain focus on educating each other on core needs first.

Idea Generation

With clarity attained regarding challenges and underlying interests, the stage is set for collaborative brainstorming—what solutions allow both parties' interests to be met?

Guidance: retain openness by avoiding yes/no responses that limit creativity here. The current single idea only merits consideration, not commitment. Instead use questions and encourage the proposal of alternatives. Say "yes and…"

to build on possibilities rather than negate them. The goal remains expanding the solution set, not fixation around one option alone.

Through mutual proposal development, ownership of solutions transfers from me versus you framings into inclusive our options. Both parties now share responsibility for eventual decisions, ensuring all feel invested in successful implementation going forward. However, idea gathering alone fails to guarantee negotiated agreements—therein lies the next critical phase.

Test for Feasibility

Any leadership negotiation effort succeeds or fails based on solution execution, not the negotiation itself. Therefore, collaboratively pressure test proposals under consideration against implementation constraints.

- How would key operational, cultural and market realities enable or obstruct this idea once enacted?

- Where might confusion, bottlenecks or communication breakdowns emerge?

- Which stakeholders merit further consultation to preempt obstacles?

Guide parties through logistics, implications and assumptions. Again encourage questioning, scenario planning and identification of failure points. Refine approaches and build contingency steps rather than debating merits alone. The goal is to jointly strengthen proposals to withstand inevitable real-world complexities. Both Saudi Aramco and Saudi citizens share responsibility for ensuring female employment policies align with religious norms and cultural nuances. All negotiating parties share accountability in surfacing potential pitfalls.

Reinforce Shared Benefits

Amidst spirited feasibility analyses, negotiators risk losing sight of the mutually beneficial goals underpinning their collaboration. Therefore, continually reinforce the shared interests or gains proposals seek to deliver to keep teams grounded in purpose. Remind parties of how solutions under consideration empower and capitalize on synergies between them.

- Why did we come together in the first place?

- What positive impacts result from our partnership?

- What can we achieve collectively that remains impossible alone?

This focus on shared benefits combats tensions that naturally arise when stress testing proposals. It also ensures teams embrace opportunities inherent in multifaceted solutions rather than retreating to simpler unilateral approaches. Partners undertaking joint infrastructure projects appreciate pooled capabilities despite added complexity. Regular reinforcement sustains faith in collaboration.

Confirm Responsibilities and Commitments

With collective buy-in secured regarding feasible solutions, conclude negotiations by confirming reciprocal expectations and commitments to drive accountability. Who owes what to whom and by when? What resources or empowerments must each party provide the other for successful execution? Insert specific review and milestone assessment dates to embed temporal accountability.

When undertaken collaboratively, negotiations can produce tremendous mutual understanding and value. But suboptimal outcomes or deteriorated relationships emerge when parties act combatively, dismissively or in self-interest alone. Clear delineation of responsibilities combats assumption gaps threatening operationalization down the line. It also holds parties answerable for upholding their end of agreements. But above all, take time to celebrate unanimous decision-making and the power of collaboration. For negotiators guided by interests over positions, mutual victory persists as the ultimate prize.

Networks in Negotiation

Many negotiators naively focus energy solely on decision makers, hoping individual authority proves sufficient for driving organizational alignment and support. However, modern entities and agreements involve intricate networks well beyond any single champion. One must identify and navigate often unspoken spheres of influence within these complex ecosystems to produce mutually beneficial partnerships poised for real-world impact.

This article provides a framework for mapping key roles within a negotiation network, determining their needs and motivations, and ultimately ensuring all critical voices join your chorus of support. With careful orchestration, these interconnected stakeholders transform from obstacles into allies clearing a path towards collaborative victory. Leadership depends on conducting this stakeholder orchestra, not just the overt soloists.

Critical Stakeholder Roles

While decision makers retain final authority, even their influence depends on the support or at least the neutrality of the following common roles found within most negotiating networks:

The Authorizer: The authorizer holds supreme formal power regarding final approvals and budget authorization. However, you may only encounter this time-constrained executive during initial scoping and final sign-offs. Even apparent authorizers cannot single handedly drive complex decisions lacking broader organizational backing. Support their leadership by jointly navigating their internal decision-making bodies.

The User/Proposer: This referral partner or prospective user constitutes your most visible ally, feeling the immediate pain or opportunity addressed by your proposed solution. Work diligently to understand their direct interests and constraints. With trust established they can serve as an invaluable coach (see below) to steer your negotiation through their own organization's needs. Their active partnership proves essential to neutralizing internal objections.

Technical Gatekeepers: While lacking overt authority, these personnel ensure compliance to policies, procedures and standards. Their focus on risk prevention blinds them to partnership upside. Finance, legal, compliance and procurement officers commonly occupy these oversight roles. Overlook them and face unexpected barriers jeopardizing deals. However, engage them directly in shaping diligence processes and they expedite rather than obstruct progress.

Informal Influencers: Beyond any formal organizational chart, certain respected advisors wield disproportionate sway on decisions through expertise others depend upon to evaluate complex matters. These management consultants, board members and technical specialists lend credibility or raise doubts behind closed doors. Identify them early and subtly enroll them as allies to validate your solution's merits amidst scrutiny.

Executive Gatekeepers: Secretaries and assistants serve as the guardians of authority, controlling access to those holding power. Earning their trust opens calendars for direct interface. However, beware of those promising connections in return for concessions—such middlemen rarely deliver. Build relationships across gates at all levels rather than depending on individual gatekeeper generosity.

Internal Coaches: Those hoping for mutual understanding between parties serve as willing coaches to guide negotiators through complex internal dynamics. They want you to avoid political pitfalls to arrive at amicable integrations. Make it easy for friendly voices behind the scenes to tout your shared interests by keeping them informed of developments. Their quiet guidance steers past looming obstacles.

Analyze to Mobilize Networks

Do not let this multiplicity of influences intimidate. Instead intentionally map your negotiating ecosystem, identify core motivations per actor, determine influence pathways, and craft messages and processes to enroll rather than overwhelm.

Start by listing major initiatives and determine all those impacting outcomes. Also assess your own organizational network, from upcoming promotions to coveted assignments. Name the parties wielding both overt and discreet influence over each decision. Avoid broad groups, identify specific personnel instead.

Next utilizing the roles above analyze individuals:

- What primary interests, pains, and constraints shape their orientation?

- Who influences their perspectives behind closed doors?

- What messages and processes could earn their support or neutrality?

Distill insights onto personalized strategy sheets to guide tailored outreach per party. Update regularly as understanding evolves. Soon patterns emerge allowing you to spot conduits for influence across scattered stakeholders.

Execute Network Negotiation Strategies

With your stakeholder ecosystem and associated maps clarified, targeted strategies emerge to guide constructive engagement:

Spot Interdependencies: Determine who influences whom early in evaluation processes. Whose validation sways technical reviewers? Which voices could undermine even vocal supporters? Map interconnections between parties to determine whose support to secure first.

Identify Shared Outcomes: Uncover interests all resonate with and reinforce these when communicating with associated parties. Emphasize how your solution powers mutual goals around innovation, efficiency, risk mitigation, etc. Alignment around common outcomes bonds disparate players.

Discretely Circle Influencers: Informal advisors require subtle but consistent information sharing to guide their recommendations. Provide insight but avoid perception of lobbying which would damage credibility. Sustained exposure shapes perspectives even among "independent" voices.

Reverse Engineer Process Flows: Work frontline colleagues to determine what objections could arise as proposals advance upstream. Prepare preemptive logical or data packages target concerns before they emerge. You now control narratives rather than responding reactively.

Neutralize Through Inclusion: Draw resisters and revisionists into consultative roles where they improve rather than undermine initiatives, benefiting through contribution. People defend what they create but attack what they lack ownership of. Proactively enroll them.

Major agreements and organizational decisions rarely rest solely with one overt champion, despite perceptions. Take time to comprehensively map complex ecosystems of formal and informal influence that factor into outcomes. Then through targeted collaboration, communication and inclusion activate this network to advocate alongside you.

When navigating intricate negotiation environments, success depends on earning support across interconnected stakeholders, not just isolated decision makers. This requires identifying key roles, understanding their varying motivations, and undertaking tailored interventions to enroll rather than confront. Approach negotiations as convening influential cohorts around common interests. Master negotiators orchestra consensus across networks laying foundations for integrated accords delivering mutual victory.

Negotiation Tactics and Strategies

Picture negotiations as complicated dances requiring coordination between partners navigating complex needs around shared goals. Missteps undermine relationships through assumptions of oppositional zero-sum games where one side must lose for the other to win. However, positive negotiations offer an alternative vision prioritizing mutual understanding, exploration of integrative solutions, and ultimately win-win progress through joint creativity benefiting all parties. This reframing empowers negotiators with practical mindsets and tactics to turn ostensible opponents into collaborators jointly invested in common success.

Cultivate Understanding First

Rather than risk stalled discussions due to differing perspectives, invest early efforts into education around respective motivations, limitations and priorities guiding negotiators. Even seemingly combative initial demands often reflect unspoken underlying needs lost amidst positional rhetoric. Therefore remain inquisitive, asking thoughtful questions that reveal core interests transcending superficial proposals. Where might potential alignment emerge amidst differences? How might you empower their success through partnership? Such mutual understanding unlocks creative problem solving benefiting both sides.

Remain Flexible Around Possibilities

Skilled negotiators know breakthrough inspiration arises through openness to alternatives, not fixation on singular solutions. Few complex accords manifest expected paths. Unpredicted setbacks necessitate mid-course corrections only enabled when parties retain line of sight regarding shared interests despite new constraints. ThereforeBrainstorm options through inclusive "us" framing that interweaves mutual gains into eventual agreements. Here flexibility and collective creativity outweigh predicts ability in producing victory.

Prioritize Relationships Within Deals

Treat negotiations as opportunities for constructive alliance building around common challenges, not self-interested contests for resources. Transactions produce contracts, but relationships enable legacies. If partnerships deteriorate despite nominal short term victories, little sustains market leadership long term other than trust born of mutual support through adversity. Therefore stand willing to revisit seemingly finalized terms to uphold relationship bonds if unexpected obstacles later emerge testing those bonds. Partners before deals.

With these mindsets established as your operating system, tangible tactics further empower positive negotiations:

Lead From Vision Over Demands

If starting talks already forecasting unacceptable concessions or rigid limits around possibilities, you anchor discussions in scarcity and opposition. Alternatively, initiate negotiations by painting an aspirational vision everyone feels motivated to manifest. Outline ultimate end states where all parties' interests align through partnership previously unimaginable alone. Now frame demands in context of enabling rather than obstructing this shared preferred future. Progress follows inspiration.

Spot Win-Win Pathways Early

The most constructive negotiations waste little time entertaining singular proposals as reason dialogues exist at all. Instead collaboratively brainstorm alternatives at outset that address core motivations simultaneously. Multiply options then identify points of leverage where minor concessions enable major mutual gains to sustain momentum. Align interests into possibilities then leverage

Convert Differences Into Process Insights

When substantial perspective gaps emerge despite best collaborative efforts, avoid framing such impasses as irreconcilable differences threatening relationships and deals. Rather utilize them as inflection points for reevaluating and optimizing the negotiation process itself. Openly assess whether the right parties are sufficiently involved, if creative spaces receive sufficient protection or if communication mechanisms empower transparency, psychological safety and trust. Jointly strengthen frameworks.

Formalize Accountability Around Reciprocity

Even mutually satisfactory terms risk fraying partnerships if not upheld equitably over time by all signatories. Therefore conclude positive negotiations by codifying clear responsibilities per party and inserting temporal milestones to enable progress assessment. Accountability ensures hospitality between negotiating boards transforms into accountability once leaving those boards. Equitable collaboration persists the potency of deals long term.

Positive negotiations arise through abandoning zero-sum assumptions of resources constraints that necessitate self-advantaged wins. With creativity, flexibility and commitment to shared interests, collaborators instead uncover unseen pathways to mutual victory through partnership. They know breakthrough inspiration depends on sustaining curiosity, openness, trust and support interpersonally between negotiating teams, not just optimal terms and concessions. Great negotiators focus first on nurturing great relationships around a common hopeful future. The rest unfolds through positivity and persistence towards goals underpinned by mutual understanding and care for collective achievement over solitary gain. This mindset charts courses for true win-win progress benefiting all parties far beyond what any could achieve alone. And therein lies the heart of masterful negotiation.

Everything Is Negotiable

Complex organizations present leaders infinite opportunities for conflict, stagnation or progress through ongoing formal and informal negotiations. Every prioritization discussion, budget allocation and partnership nurtures potential discord or collective achievement depending on navigation. Rather than limit ambitions based on constrained resources, fixed mindsets or positional politics, collaborative negotiation introduces possibilities otherwise dismissed as non-starters based on initial appearances. Master negotiators know everything merits explorative discussion.

Question Perceived Constraints

Many negotiations flounder before conversations even begin due to anchoring around assumed limitations rather than jointly questioning viability of seemingly set variables. Leaders instill silence around protected priorities stifling collaborative challenges regarding mutually suboptimal arrangements.

However, are self-imposed constraints actually mandated or simply comfortable? For instance, direct compensation may be contractually fixed, but bonus structures and ancillary perks introduce flexible incentives empowering across organizations. Get curious about broader possibilities before assuming or enforcing rigidity.

Uncover What Motivates Priorities

Just as compensation elements enjoy negotiable flexibility, all strategic priorities reflect underlying interests driving leaders' commitment more than the initiatives themselves. Budget disputes or departmental conflicts often shadow diversity, equity and inclusion misalignments, challenges around succession planning gaps or lurking skill deficiencies rather than purely funding discrepancies. Rediscovering fundamental motivations opens imaginative win-win solutions obscured when masked as positional standoffs over resources. Reveal then elevate aspirations.

Engage Multiple Perspectives

Entropy plagues insular negotiations as discussions circle familiar participants invested in preserving status quos. However, injecting historically excluded voices, marginalized viewpoints and unconventional provocateurs exposes overlooked interdependencies and sparks fresh ideation. Rather than debate arrangements between established poles, engage unfamiliar agents of change to challenge paradigms. Through multiplicity, discover viability where once ruled impossible.

Empower Decentralized Innovation

Top-down negotiations naturally focus on optimizing constraints around current-state limitations often protecting legacy arrangements favoring incumbents. However, equitable next generation solutions demand pushing peripheries of possibility through autonomous team empowerment uncovering breakthroughs aligning to bolder ambition. Therefore, balance corporate negotiations with seeded funding, structural autonomy and network access accelerating grassroots experiments around organization-wide challenges once deemed intractable at scale. Let many flowers bloom.

Effective leadership negotiations demand questioning perceived realities previously taken as set limitations on ambition. Everything merits collaborative discussion when envisioning expansive possibilities and engaging diverse perspectives. Where prior generation leaders entrenched assumptions, deliberate ambiguity now invites perpetual innovation.

Key Takeaways and Final Thoughts on Negotiations

- bilizing intricate networks of formal and informal influence proves foundational for securing organizational alignment

- Embrace ambiguity and open-ended creativity over constraints to reveal breakthrough possibilities beyond initial assumptions

- Prioritizing understanding and relationships over transactions protects partnerships when inevitabilities test agreements

- Question rigid limitations on resources and priorities to empower decentralized innovation around once intractable challenges

The Power of Shared Possibility

Negotiations persist as intricate dances requiring coordination and creativity between partners navigating complex needs around shared goals. Yet when undertaken through a spirit of mutual collaboration more akin to open-ended design thinking than zero-sum contests over limited resources, negotiations unlock possibility and progress benefiting entire organizations and partnerships exponentially more than any outcome achievable by isolated parties alone. This promise positions positive negotiation as a cornerstone leadership capability distinguishing visionaries who transform constraints into springboards for previously unimaginable potential.

Master negotiators invest in inquisitive discovery of underlying interests, informal networks of influence and ambitious visions for integrative progress years before formalizing transactional terms. They know conversations produce springboards into futures far beyond what current limitations supposedly allow. Every budget merits reimagining, every priority warrants revaluation and every partnership beckons reinvigoration when leaders instill a collective commitment to shared possibility over constraints.

But possibility only manifests through hard work turning inspiration into accountability. Creative agreements require clearly delineated reciprocal expectations, transparent progress indicators and resilient communication channels that sustain partnerships long after handshakes. And rather than centralize negotiations, visionary leadership empowers decentralized teams closest to operational complexities to redefine the scope of what challenges merit direct disruption. The resultant explosions of grassroots experimentation yield locally-sourced breakthroughs never visible from executive suites alone.

What once seemed implausible alone suddenly appears inevitable together when leaders nurture cultures embracing positive negotiation's promise of progress through shared possibility, accountability and decentralized innovation. But does your organization cling to constrained assumptions and transactional views limiting ambition? If so, what currently deemed impossibilities might collaboration reveal as low hanging fruits begging plucking? Now those opportunities call for your leadership. Shall we begin?

Chapter Eight

Professional Networking

Networking is often viewed as an uncomfortable chore rather than a rewarding endeavor with immense upside potential. How can rising leaders adopt an empowered mindset and leverage networking to amplify their impact? By reframing networking as the cultivation of meaningful connections, leaders can unlock countless personal and professional benefits.

At its core, a professional network simply represents the web of relationships leaders develop based on shared interests, experiences and expertise. While many instinctually cringe at the notion of traditional networking events with overly-eager attendees aggressively pitching business cards, a network can manifest both organically or intentionally in a multitude of formats. Leaders might connect with an industry peer at a convention session that sparks an inspiring brainstorming session afterwards. Or a friendly conversation at a charity gala may surface a promising partnership opportunity. The advent of digital networking on platforms like LinkedIn also allows connections to form across the globe based on shared vision and values rather than physical proximity and chance encounters.

However, some leaders hesitate engaging in networking, worrying that uncomfortable small talk or self-promotional conversations feel inauthentic. Instead, approach networking as a learning opportunity with peers to discover hidden synergies and possibilities through genuine human connections. When a leader approaches conversations with genuine curiosity about the passions and purpose behind each individual they meet, powerful relationships are more likely to emerge.

The benefits of expanding networks are multi-faceted. First, connecting with professionals across diverse industries grants invaluable access to new ideas and alternative growth strategies a leader may not uncover in their daily environment. Enriching one's perspective allows for greater creativity and innovation leadership. Second, networking establishes a leader's visibility and sphere of influence, allowing them to achieve bigger goals by accessing a wider pool of potential collaborators and resources. Leaders able to form strategic partnerships through aligned networks achieve exponentially more than they ever could accomplish in isolation.

Finally, networking serves a key role in talent recruitment and retention efforts. With trends like "The Great Resignation" allowing top performers their choice of employer, many gravitate towards purpose-driven leaders and resonant missions they discover through their networks. Likewise, when roles need to be filled, leaders can leverage their connections to rapidly source ideal candidates through recommendations.

While cultivating a powerful professional network requires concerted effort, leaders will reap rewards for decades to come. As management expert Ron Cross advises professionals: "Be genuine in your communications, offer help to others with no expected return, and watch your network grow in both size and richness." The connections formed today may well support leaders in landing their next career opportunities, attracting top-tier talent, sparking global innovations and beyond – but first leaders must open their minds and hearts to the infinite potential already surrounding them in their networks.

Establishing a Professional Network

While many understand the immense value of networking in theory, far fewer are able to effectively leverage connections to create tangible career opportunities and long-term competitive advantage. This guide explores pragmatic strategies rising professionals and executives can implement to foster robust professional networks that facilitate career advancement, recruit top talent, spark innovative partnerships and accelerate impact.

Assess Your Goals and Passions

When beginning your networking journey, first reflect inwardly to gain clarity on your true professional passions, capabilities and aspirations independent of current job titles or assigned responsibilities. While some leaders feel anchored to a particular industry or role due to experience or education, envision how your innate skills and interests might translate into adjacent sectors. For example, transferrable competencies like complex problem solving, empathy and communication lend themselves well to consulting and human resources fields regardless of previous specialty area. Additionally, reflect on parts of your existing role that energize you most along with causes you feel passionate about contributing to. Understanding internal motivations helps identify networking opportunities offering fulfillment beyond surface-level career advancement.

Research Individuals Who Can Impact Your Aims

With clarity of professional purpose and aspirations, meticulously research industries and organizations aligned to your goals to pinpoint influential individuals well-positioned to help you achieve them. Seek those spearheading cutting-edge initiatives or commanding extensive networks themselves. While blind online invitations often go overlooked, customized messaging referencing an individual's accomplishments and expertise immediately captures attention and conveys sincere interest in mutual value creation. Even small actions like engaging content can organically forge strategic connections.

Look Within Your Current Circle

Scan your existing connections for any warm introductions to pertinent companies or leaders within them. A personal reference acts as a credible stamp of approval, exponentially increasing response rates compared to cold outreach. Discuss your targeted networking goals transparency with past managers, colleagues and even university alumni in leadership positions to activate support. You may be surprised just how willing seasoned professionals are to guide emerging talent when approached constructively.

Initiate Engagement

Once identifying networking targets, craft customized communication highlighting overlap in values, interests and professional pursuits. Outreach should be specific enough to demonstrate awareness of an individual's unique accomplishments and contributions while broad enough to allow natural dialogue flow regarding aligning opportunities. The most meaningful professional connections develop gradually through ongoing dialogue so avoid "overselling" to let relationships progress organically. With responsive parties, suggest meeting to explore synergies.

Add Value from the Outset

Approach new networking connections seeking to add value, not extract it. Research indicates that givers accrue exponential returns in business networks compared to strict takers. Thoughtfully consider how your skills, experiences and network might support another's goals prior to requesting assistance. This seed of goodwill often motivates reciprocation down the line. Even small gestures like sharing an article or connection demonstrates proactive support.

Align on Next Steps

Before concluding networking conversations, outline concrete next steps, such as meeting again or coordinating an introduction. Vague intentions rarely materialize into collaborative action whereas clear commitments necessitate follow through. Maintain momentum by scheduling future touchpoints during initial exchanges or recapping agreed action items in thank you correspondence.

Expand Your Circle Continuously

Make network expansion a perpetual professional priority rather than a sporadic occurrence only when changing roles or seeking opportunities. Set periodic goals to connect with several new contacts within your industry monthly. Sustain existing relationships through regular check-ins even without urgent updates. You never know when a conversation with an old colleague may unlock unanticipated doors so consistently nurture connections.

While networking may seem like an uncomfortable distraction from pressing daily workflows, prioritizing meaningful relationship building with influential professionals ultimately pays long-term career dividends. Consider it a wise investment in your personal infrastructure to support current and future success. Maintain genuine curiosity about the needs and offerings of others while proactively sharing your own and professionally lucrative collaborations will naturally emerge.

Expanding your professional network may appear an imposing undertaking initially but incremental effort applied consistently over years cultivates community clout and career propulsion far exceeding isolated gains. Authentically engage professionals aligned to your values and aspirations by adding value, establishing follow-up commitments and continually expanding your circle of trust. The positive compounding returns of such strategic networking will serve rising leaders and seasoned executives alike in unlocking increased impact, innovation and fulfillment throughout their journeys. Now fully equipped with strategies to establish robust connectivity, dare to take the first step toward unprecedented opportunity by simply reaching out. The only thing you have to lose is possibility itself.

Building Trust in Professional Relationships

While leaders readily acknowledge trust's foundational role theoretically, far fewer devote consistent effort toward nurturing interpersonal credibility and intimacy underpinning the deepest professional bonds over time.

This guide delves into the psychology of trust to empower rising professionals and executives alike to foster robust relationships rooted in mutual understanding and aligned vision. While handing out business cards or attending networking happy hours may result in superficial associations, leaders must invest concentrated effort exploring common values, demonstrating genuine care and minimizing risk perceptions to transform promising connections into enduring allies.

Differentiate Network Depth from Breadth

A leader's network value correlates directly to trust and influence rather than solely the number of relationships maintained. Simply assembling extensive contact lists or LinkedIn connections devoid of emotional intimacy breeds networks as ineffective as Rolodexes gathering dust, with communication requests ignored and diaries perpetually full upon meeting requests. True network potency stems from a handful of deep relationships offer mutual support during victories and vulnerabilities alike versus scores of surface-level bonds.

Rather than fixating on continually expanding networks' breadth, audit existing connections' depth periodically by asking:

- How quickly does this contact respond to outreach?

- Have we supported each other's stretch projects and personal development goals?

- Do we confide in one another regarding situational uncertainties?

- Would we collaborate again based on previous partnership fulfillment?

Relationships scoring lower warrant further trust building so leaders should redirect networking energy accordingly until all connections feel mutually enriching.

Anchor Bonds in Shared Purpose and Values

Trust forms most swiftly when parties share aligned purpose, values and outlooks fundamentally, whether regarding business growth or community impact. When professionals speak the same aspirational language and exude infectious enthusiasm towards their work, barriers to collaboration erode organically even without extensive past dealings. Seek opportunities to engage prospective allies about ambitious visions or values core to their personal missions to establish immediate resonance on emotional levels, where authentic relationships take root.

For example, an executive equally passionate about championing minority advancement and an nonprofit leader dedicated to equality might sense an instant kinship through shared values prioritizing inclusive empowerment despite operating in wholly distinct sectors. When parties lead with soul rather than roles, trust flows freely.

Build Intimacy Through Vulnerability

Resist confining new networking conversations purely to stiff professional terrain. While discussing high-level goals and limitations surrounding work projects may convey competence and authority initially, exclusively projecting our public persona inhibits emotional intimacy underpinning the most fulfilling professional bonds. Demonstrating authentic vulnerability by sharing personal challenges overcome, lessons learned by mistakes made or simply proud parenting moments builds affinity and signals leaders' humanity. Reciprocity typically inspires connections to reciprocate in kind.

Leaders should also guide discussions covering common experiences, passions or connections kindling a sense of community through shared identity markers like university alumni status or hometowns. Thoughtfully listening and responding to personal anecdotes forges genuine care and concern.

Seed Early Wins to Gain Credibility

Commence budding professional relationships focused on collaborator needs before your own to seed goodwill prompting reciprocity down the road. For instance, you might introduce a promising new connection to an industry peer who faced similar scaling challenges or share an insightful article addressing questions surfaced in initial exchanges. These proactive signals of support absent immediate desired return demonstrate selfless commitment to mutual success.

Also propose quick collaborative actions clearly benefiting counterparts after just brief interactions, such as coordinating peer mentoring circles or compiling trend reports. Consistently achieving small but meaningful contributions toward someone's ambitions earns credibility critical for establishing trust in interdependent environments before parties commit to more resource-intensive collaboration mandating unwavering confidence in follow-through.

Mitigate Risk Perceptions Through Clarity

When exploring potential collaborations with those lacking existing loyalty through past projects, thoughtfully evaluate possibilities from their self-oriented perspective. What workload, opportunity costs and political capital must this executive risk by supporting my initiative? Does involvement expose them to criticism if not executed flawlessly? Then devise strategies to minimize perceived downside, clearly conveying why participating promotes their goals through easily understandable logic.

Leaders able to effectively decrease the subjective risk, effort and uncertainty colleagues must accept to partner expand pools of willing contributors dramatically not through coercion but aligned incentive structures. Maintaining a self-centered stance while attempting to construct trusting networks is para-doxical so continually reframe shared interests.

In summary, trust remains the bedrock every impactful professional network and collaborative team rests upon but establishing meaningful connection re-quires much more than exchanging business cards with high volume contacts. Devote time delving below the surface through emotional intimacy, support absent strings and upside focus to transform promising relationships into pow-erful catalysts driving exponential returns for all parties over the long-term. The past era's transaction-based networking tactics must give way to service-centered relationship building strategies prioritizing trust at the core. After all, we attract who and what we are so our networks ultimately reflect our innermost priorities – do yours center on self or shared success?

How to Leverage Your Network

An expansive professional network marks the defining difference separating those thriving in fulfilling careers from others stagnated in place, unaware of new openings or lacking influencers to endorse their potential. Yet while most recognize referrals from a robust network as essential for accessing life-changing opportunities, far fewer devote effort effectively cultivating, engaging and stew-arding connections granting that competitive edge.

This guide outlines field-tested networking strategies enabling professionals to transform dormant contacts into active advocates catapulting their aspirations. You will learn to nurture relationships rooted in mutual support rather than extraction, converge digital networking with interpersonal engagement and continually sow seeds of goodwill through generosity. Master these techniques for enriching your network and unlock unprecedented career capital.

Identify Your Career Goals and Skills

The foundation to maximizing any network's strategic value begins with clari-fying your true professional passions, capabilities and objectives. This enables targeting outreach to connections able to directly enable your goals through tailored counsel, collaborations or introductions.

Start by contemplating what draws you to your work intrinsically beyond extrinsic motivations like compensation or prestige. How do you hope your efforts impact community or customer experiences? What underlying motivations and strengths fuel your performance? Do aspects of your current role fail to ignite your drive?

Next, revisit the unique combination of transferable abilities, specialized technical fluencies and soft skills that set you apart from peers. Do others routinely praise your empathy, creativity or communication talents? What accomplishments feel most proud of? Any expertise gaps requiring development?

Having defined your professional purpose and abilities, contemplate specific positional aspirations you're progressing towards short and long term. Perhaps you aim to manage a larger team in coming years or transition industries completely. Outlining hopes beyond next quarter's quotas grounds strategic networking.

Share Knowledge and Learn Continuously

Resist compartmentalizing your network contacts into mere transactional stepping stones toward self-focused aims without concern for reciprocal value. Instead, approach relationships as rich opportunities for mutual growth and fulfillment.

Proactively share industry insights, resources and introductions to contacts where appropriate, understanding rising tides lift all ships. If a peer oversees launching a new product, send motivational notes and annotate spreadsheets to accelerate their success. When colleagues face steep learning curves adjusting to technologies disrupting traditional workflows, volunteer digital literacy coaching.

Networks represent communities so contribute actively; share personal career lessons learned overcoming prior missteps and celebrate peers' victories as your own. Listen attentively to uncover hidden gems of wisdom from unexpected sources. The savviest leaders remain lifelong students.

Leverage Conferences and Events

Industry gatherings offer unmatched networking efficiency to interact with hundreds of aligned professionals in brief windows, but only when appropriately strategized. Begin researching registered attendee lists and panelist bios as early as possible, noting peers you hope to meet. If specific executives prove unavoidable but share common education or regional backgrounds, highlight such touchpoints in initial exchanges to break the ice.

At venues, balance asserting your voice confidently during group discussions with graciously ceding the floor to allow others spotlight moments conveying subject mastery or passion. Express genuine interest in learning colleagues' career journeys before promoting personal accomplishments. Following dialogue, suggest meeting later to unpack insights further while they remain fresh rather than attempting to exchange business cards while rushing towards next sessions.

Most critically, dedicate effort maintaining periodic contact with new connections afterward rather than allowing inspiration that day alone catalyze your follow-through.

Curate Your Digital Identity

While face-to-face networking remains ideal for relationship building nuance, thoughtfully managing digital footprints greatly bolsters tangible opportunities by efficiently signaling professional capabilities to target audiences.

For example, cultivating an aesthetically polished LinkedIn presence highlighting career milestones, community leadership and recommendations attracts recruiting decision-makers even passively. Similarly, commenting on industry leaders' blog posts or podcasts showcases subject matter expertise publically.

Social channels also enable interacting directly with colleagues posting career updates or content you find compelling. Beyond cursory likes, contribute value by asking thoughtful questions, offering resources or introducing them to contacts that would benefit from knowing them. Relationships thrive with consistent digital nurturing between in-person touchpoints.

Seed Career Conversations Organically

Rather than viewing professional small talk as means to a transactional end, recognize mundane conversations' latent potential. Displaying authentic interest in peers' lives and families, commiserating good-naturedly about office quirks and celebrating shared passions transports interactions to human levels where camaraderie naturally takes root. These seeds of rapport blossom into career alliances indirectly over years.

Consider chatting affably about a colleague's favorite sports team and later receiving an unsolicited referral to their spouse's thriving company aligned with your goals or playfully debating pizza toppings resulting in improved collaboration on difficult projects. Once establishing mutual trust and care beyond professional domains through lighthearted interactions, associates eagerly support your pursuits sensing kinship rather than obligation.

Keep Your Circle Close

Accept that nurturing a handful of profoundly meaningful relationships proves exponentially more valuable than building extensive superficial networks where contacts remain near-strangers. Rather than continually expanding networks' breadth neglecting depth, devote effort strengthening existing bonds through shared experiences.

For instance, passing two hours monthly to catch up with a former manager still fondly remembering your contributions seeds immense career capital compared to one-off coffee meetings with a dozen casual peers offering temporarily helpful advice before fading from memory. Relationships centered on authenticity and service cultivate blossoming careers; transactional associations deliver fleeting returns.

The Connections You Make Mirror Who You Are

Finally, remember that throughout your networking journey, the character and intentions put forth attract like-minded individuals. Lead with generosity, learn from wisdom in unlikely places and direct others toward opportunity whenever able, and your community will soon overflow with allies rallying around shared ambition. While mastering the techniques detailed here accelerates success, living your purpose seeds fulfilling collaborations serving far beyond yourself. Now expand your mind to the abundance of support surrounding you and take the first step toward new horizons by simply reaching out. The only variable limiting your impact remains your imagination so boldly connect.

Key Takeaways and Final Thoughts on Professional Networking

Key Takeaways:

- Authentically connecting with others by leading with generosity and service lays the foundation for powerful professional relationships and expanded career opportunities.

- Invest time understanding contacts' unique goals and perspectives to uncover shared interests and potential synergies for collaboration.

- Continually nurture connections through consistent communication and actively supporting their interests without expectation of immediate returns.

- Conferences and events provide efficiency in expanding networks, but follow-up determines actual return on investments.

- Curate digital footprints highlighting capabilities and signaling possibilities to prospective allies.

- Look beyond roles and credentials to make personalized connections on fundamental values and passions fueling people's dedication.

Building Relationships for Mutual Success

The depth of leaders' professional networks marks the defining difference between those seizing new opportunities and those stagnating in place. Yet while most readily acknowledge referrals from robust networks prove essential for advancement, far fewer devote effort effectively cultivating, engaging and stewarding the connections underpinning their success.

This guide outlined proven strategies enabling professionals to transform dormant contacts into active advocates ready to elevate their aspirations. By leading with generosity rather than extracting value, understanding individuals beyond credentials and continually nurturing bonds through shared experiences, mutual prosperity emerges.

While conferences and events increase networking efficiency, follow-up determines actual returns on investments. Curating digital footprints signals capabilities to prospective allies passively by highlighting career milestones, community leadership and peer recommendations. Look beyond formal roles and recognize the potential in every personal connection. Small talk today may open doors to undiscovered possibilities tomorrow when foundations of authentic caring lay beneath.

The future remains unwritten and opportunities arising each day flow directly from the network already surrounding professionals eager to lift others higher. Now expand your mind to the abundance of support already available and take the first step toward new horizons by simply reaching out. The only variable limiting your impact remains your imagination so boldly connect with open heart.

What existing connections in your network might appreciate receiving a brief check-in from you today? How could you creatively add value to them without expecting anything directly in return? By seeding such sparks of potential and goodwill through consistent effort over years, the harvest of new career heights your network yields may surprise you exponentially.

Chapter Nine

Working with Senior Management

Organizational hierarchies inherently create distance between senior leaders and frontline employees. Though top executives shape company strategy and direction, they depend on insights from all levels to make informed decisions. Bridging this gap requires understanding the motivations driving leadership and learning to communicate in ways that resonate.

By aligning your approach and mindset with senior management, you gain invaluable visibility that accelerates your impact and career progression. This article explores practical strategies for earning the trust and respect of organizational leaders by speaking their language. With concerted preparation and an empowering perspective, any motivated employee can positively influence top-down decisions.

Understanding the View from the Top

The foremost obstacle in connecting with senior management is perspective. Executives spend their days in meetings, reviewing reports, developing long-term plans, and putting out fires. They operate in a world of abstraction - far removed from daily operations.

Consequently, leadership obsessively seeks insights on ground realities. They need your help piercing the veil of bureaucracy and formal processes that sanitizes the information reaching them. This rare view into daily operations and customer interactions makes your observations invaluable.

But sharing raw experiences causes communication breakdowns. Leaders speak a different language, prioritizing macro trends, cross-functional impacts, and strategic responses. Effectively conveying micro observations in this macro context is an acquired skill.

The translation burden falls on frontline employees seeking to share revelations with senior management. Organizational psychologist Edgar Schein's research on subcultures provides a useful framework for analysis. Apply his concepts of espoused values versus underlying assumptions to decode leadership thought patterns.

This theory deconstructs the aspirational goals trumpeted in company promotions and the unquestioned worldviews that actually drive behavior. Learning to navigate this nuance helps package your messages for maximum leadership buy-in.

Preparing Your Perspective

Credibly commenting on strategy requires understanding leadership priorities. Thorough preparation entails investigating the burning issues occupying executive bandwidth. This enables framing frontline experiences as solutions instead of complaints.

Start by identifying upcoming leadership decisions and challenges. Talk to administrators, analyze meeting agendas, and read the latest annual reports. Establish the context before finalizing the content of your message.

Next, liaise with managers to clarify senior management's preferred data formats. Learn to lead with high-level impacts before providing granular detail.

Quantify insights whenever possible using the performance indicators that leadership tracks.

Finally, rehearse responses to likely leader questions with the help of a mentor. Brainstorm to predict the information they will find most interesting and concerning. Practice summarizing key takeaways to prepare soundbites when opportunities for face time are limited.

With this aligned frame of reference, you can share the same realities through a lens tailored to leadership priorities. Now the challenge becomes earning their attention long enough to relay those insights.

Building Personal Credibility

Influencing leadership decisions requires first influences their perceptions of you. Every interaction, however fleeting builds or erodes your credibility. Earning respect requires consistently demonstrating trustworthiness.

According to Wharton professor Adam Grant's research, trust emerges from three key behaviors:

- Transparent communication

- Embracing opportunities to help

- Admitting and learning from mistakes.

Focus on embodying these traits in all your interactions.

Transparency requires sharing the unvarnished truth while being solution-focused. Frame problems with proposed responses to show you are invested in driving progress. Leaders seek agents of change not passive purveyors of complaints.

The desire to help means proactively seeking opportunities to contribute, even if they fall outside formal responsibilities. Discretionary effort displays commitment to collective objectives over personal status. It distinguishes passionate undertakings from transactional jobs.

Everyone makes mistakes but having the courage to acknowledge them transforms failures into lessons. Honest accountability demonstrates resilience essential for leadership roles. It also allows quickly correcting course instead of doubling down or covering up errors.

Living these principles earns you recognition as someone willing to speak truth to power respectfully but unafraid of hard conversations. Leadership places immense trust in such confidantes to provide unfiltered perspectives. This shifts discussions from speculation to grounded realities enabling data-based decisions.

Acting the Part in the Room

Earning a seat at the leadership table requires credibly filling the part once you get there. Presence conveys authority. The way you carry yourself while sharing messages signals your depth of conviction.

Exude quiet confidence rooted in preparation instead of bravado. Resist urges to fill silence by speaking slowly after questions. Thoughtful pauses demonstrate carefully contemplating responses, not lack of substance.

Channel nervous energy into active listening which makes others feel valued. Remember details leadership shares to reference later, demonstrating genuine interest in their perspective. This establishes rapport and distinguishes engaging conversations from one-sided lobbying.

When disagreeing avoid combative language that puts leaders on the defensive. Know when to stop pressing points and compromise to preserve political capital for bigger battles. Achieving influence requires balancing conviction with judicious pushback informed by group dynamics knowledge.

Organizational hierarchies stem from necessities in coordinating large collectives though they inherently limit information flows. But thought diversity oils the gears of progress. So leaders seek out frontline observers as their eyes and ears. Shared honestly while upholding respect enables combining big-picture thinking with ground realities.

This symbiotic partnership requires effort from both sides. Leadership must value on-the-ground experiences while employees need translating insights into the strategic vernacular. Preparation and mindset shifts can bridge perspectives. When done effectively this knowledge exchange becomes a competitive advantage propelling careers and fueling organizational advancement.

The divide between the C-suite and customer-facing roles is imposing but navigable. Sweat the small stuff in your preparations to seem strategic in the room. Build trust through principled interactions over time. Soon you will find leaders not only listening when you speak but seeking you out.

How Senior Leaders Approach Problems

Managers often view executive thinking patterns through simplistic lenses. The common perception of the CEO painstakingly analyzing quantitative data to make rational choices underestimates the complexity behind high-level decision making. This article explores the cognitive priorities and processes genuinely shaping the executive perspective.

By highlighting the differences between senior leader mental models and classical strategy formulations, these insights reframe understanding effective management practices. Beyond skill-building, they reveal the mindset shifts essential for transitioning from functional roles to general management responsibilities.

Rethinking the Rational Model

The logical decision-making process begins by clearly defining organizational goals, assessing current realities, formulating options, evaluating probable outcomes, deciding on an optimal path forward, and finally executing the chosen strategy. This sequence implies clinical objectivity applied one discretely defined problem at a time.

Yet in practice, senior executive thinking diverges sharply from this orderly approach. Real-world constraints on time and political capital make purely reason-based choices untenable. Instead, leaders rely extensively on intuitional judgement honed through experience to navigate ambiguity.

Furthermore, strategic development occurs simultaneously across interconnected domains rather than in isolated silos. Thisparallel processing of interlinked problemsrunning in the background differentiates executive thinking patterns from compartmentalized logic trees.

Senior Management Core Concerns

Effective leadership hinges on addressing overarching concerns consuming senior thought according to studies. This report examines proven techniques for assisting executives through focusing efforts on their foremost priorities.

1. *Crafting organizational and interpersonal processes:* Research shows managers dedicate significant attention to establishing high-functioning processes across levels. Streamlining workflows incorporates staff input, optimizing contributions according to aptitudes. Centralizing expertise bolsters efficiency and strategic flexibility.

2. *Anticipating Broader Shifts and Uncertainties:* Executives likewise ruminate on exigent transitions and potential disruptions. Anticipating macroeconomic patterns, competitor maneuvers, and emergent technologies preserves advantage. Scenario planning mitigates risks through distributed consideration of alternatives.

3. *Addressing Concerns Through Process Facilitation:* Assist executives by spearheading process audits and coordination to minimize distractions from their supervision. Conduct stakeholder interviews iden-

tifying bottlenecks; pilot optimizations guided by productivity metrics. Provide regular forecasts and risk assessments supporting strategic foresight.

Busy leaders have a lot on their minds each day. Research shows they often think most about big picture concerns and uncertainties. While specifics still matter, higher level issues take up more mental energy. Experts say helping leaders with big concerns reduces strain. Focusing work on their top priorities lightens leaders' load. Things run smoother when others clear roadblocks through improved systems. This lets leaders spend brainpower where it's needed most.

Finding ways to streamline workflows helps. Talking to staff identifies clogged spots. Testing fixes makes work better using metrics. Keeping leaders updated on longer term risks and changes also lifts weight off. Concentrating efforts upstream makes downstream run smooth. Leaders then have bandwidth for important strategic pondering. Working as a team to solve problems collaboratively lifts load all around. Leaders lead best when supported to focus where they add maximum value.

Process Preoccupation

Senior management thinking fixates on building frameworks to coordinate collective actions for achieving goals. Executives continuously contemplate mobilization challenges: Whose support is essential? Who should be brought in at what stage? What signals will various sequencing send?

For instance, when considering potential compensation redesign, structural realignments, or plant closures, the foremost thoughts relate to managing engagement, alignment, and change management. The substance of decisions remains background context.

This process obsession stems from the direct dependence of leaders on enabling others to enact their vision. Unlike specialized experts who derive authority from domain mastery, general managers must incentivize cooperation through networked influence.

Hence thought processes concentrate on motivating organizational energy towards priority outcomes through interpersonal connections. Who thinks what and how they can be brought around becomes the central preoccupation.

Overriding Concerns

In contrast with the popular image of executives continually juggling diverse strategic and operational considerations, senior leader cognition consolidates around one or two broad overriding concerns for extended periods.

These dominant themes capture complex multifaceted priorities like reorganizing structure, turning around performance, or driving culture change. With steadfast focus, leaders then evaluate all activities through this singular lens above immediate tactical concerns.

For instance, the first 100 days agenda of new executives usually coalesces around large scale transformation like correcting underperformance across businesses. This all-consuming drive subordinates individual functional metrics to the overriding turnaround imperative.

The cognitive consolidation frees bandwidth for managing the interconnected web of tactical decisions required to progress the dominant concern. The singular clarity of purpose minimizes conflicting priorities that paralyze wider perspectives. It enables framing choices through a consistent criterion.

Making Strategic Progress

Sustainable progress necessitates calculated yet flexible decision sequences according to research. This report examines leadership models navigating multifaceted transformations through controlled experimentation.

Rather than exhaustive pre-execution planning, experts advise interleaving analysis and contained implementations. Initial alterations reveal nuances guiding successive customization until visions materialize. Outcomes adjust expectations versus rigid presumptions.

Considering interdependencies, leaders strategically sequence decisions accounting for ramifications across initiatives. Instead of compartmentalized issues, a holistic balancing of interacting uncertainties yields balanced progress. Studying cascading impacts optimizes cooperative gains.

Leaders enhance understanding through judicious experimentation guided by realities over rigid formulations. Testing hypotheses under stipulations furnishes learning surpassing analysis alone. Strategic trial design and review supports agile evidence-based progress according to emergent realities.

Progress hinges on iterative decision cycles incorporating contingencies according to research. Leaders facilitate sustainable transformations through portfolio optimization and controlled trials revealing policy insights. Strategic agility cultivates cooperative advancements adapting to realities versus predetermined presumptions.

Implications for Transitioning Leaders

These insights on senior management thinking have profound implications for rising executives. Aspiring leaders must reorient thought processes towards enabling large scale coordination.

Four shifts stand out in particular:

1. Develop networked influence across functions

2. Focus more on aligning people than perfecting analysis

3. Frame specific goals within broader overriding quests

4. Make progress through intertwined attempts rather than solitary solutions

Rather than expecting systemic change through individual contribution, executives architect collective transformation through connections. They inspire progress by concentrating attention and passion towards shared overriding concerns.

Classical strategy models underestimate the complexity of general management. Rational choices dissolve amidst ambiguity and influence constraints requiring senior leaders to set direction through broader themes. Progress emerges through coordinated momentum built by concentrating organizational energy towards targeted concerns.

Executive thinking interweaves meta-goals, interpersonal processes and ever-evolving attempts into an integrated effort. By recognizing these realities, rising managers can align better with leadership to enable success. The ability to orient others towards necessary transformations distinguishes effective general managers.

Strategies for Engaging with Senior Leaders

Large organizations run on ideas as much as operations. Generating change requires capturing leadership attention with compelling visions. However, credibility gaps arise between frontline observations and the executive suite. Bridging this chasm demands tactical engagement relying on empathy, evidence, and concision.

This guide compiles field-tested techniques for effectively advocating proposals to senior decision-makers. By understanding leader psychology, speaking their language, and upholding respect, employees at all levels can positively shape organizational direction. Progress rests on clearly communicating with those empowered to enable action.

Have an Informed Opinion

voicing views signals confidence and capability. But as volume rises with hierarchy, opinions require grounding in analysis, coherently communicated. Leaders seek informed counsel rather than redundant confirmation. Unique yet rational perspectives reveal care and capability.

Recommendations demand thoughtful rationale explaining their role in company objectives. Blind assertions waste opportunity and patience. Executives respectfully pressure-test proposals expecting substantive rejoinders. Success means quickly responding to scrutiny by linking suggestions to financial impact and competitive advantage.

When aligned with leadership goals, opinions become catalysts rather than complaints. Effective framing invites constructive debate around mutual purpose rather than defensive posturing. Consider all sides to provide solutions attuned to complex constraints facing executives. Progress happens collaboratively.

See Leaders as Human

The C-suite seems rarefied air where inscrutable forces determine fates. Yet inhabiting powerful roles still leaves individuals subject to universal social and psychological tendencies even amidst high stakes. Understanding this humanity enables connecting genuinely.

All people possess fundamental desires for respect, belonging, autonomy and competence. When threatened, universal defense mechanisms like avoidance and denial manifest, even in executives. Leaders equally experience insecurities when asked to shift entrenched mindsets. Empathetically approaching discomforts around uncertainty unlocks willingness to engage.

With compassionate listening, discuss experiences to establish shared understanding around customer emotions. Leaders should describe frustrations felt during their worst service interactions and envision the alternative. Connect C-suite humanity to realities of all people relying on the organization to meet needs. This grounds proposals in tangible contexts and makes abstract aspirations personally relatable.

Appreciate Strategic Perspectives

Specialization breeds granular views that lose sight of contextual interdependencies. As responsibilities expand, leaders prioritize broader implications over isolated outputs. Grasping this wider lens helps frame suggestions strategically.

When presenting ideas, outline market positioning considerations and competitors likely to react. Discuss implementation challenges spanning functions like supply chain, marketing and human resources. Explore alignment with cultures and values impacting adoption. Thinking cross-functionally demonstrates systematic evaluation vital for large-scale change.

Leadership responsibilities transcend technical prowess. Executives excel by enabling collective action towards common cause. Support wider objectives through flexibility meeting integrated requirements. Welcome curiosity uncovering deeper dimensions of proposals.

Be Clear and Concise

Assume senior leaders possess full schedules before requesting time. Place importance on their attention by meticulously preparing tight arguments. Demonstrate respect through brevity and clarity conveying coherence quickly.

Start by aligning suggestions to current leadership priorities revealed in public communications and interviews. Then connect proposals directly to key performance indicators influencing these priorities like revenue, market share and profitability.

Prepare to flex the flow of conversation, adjusting to feedback and probing questions. Smoothly guide dialogue back on track rather than rigidly adhering to script. Convey confidence through poise in the face of scrutiny. Leaders favor those able to hold their own through informed pushback while avoiding defensive postures.

Lead with Financial Impact

Capitalism concentrates power with those controlling resources. While social and environmental concerns increasingly enter boardroom discussions, financial returns remain the decision-making anchor. Income enables impact.

Solid numbers validating concepts demonstrate diligence and strategic alignment. Model impacts on key ratios and performance thresholds over relevant timeframes. Know details on measurement systems, past results and future projections. Admit limitations while ensuring believability within reasonable confidence levels.

Leverage pilots demonstrating potential when forecasts contain uncertainty. Seek signoff implementing controlled experiments minimizing resource requirements while generating initial data. Small wins build confidence in wider rollouts requiring greater investment. Right size requests to balance boldness with achievability.

Executive advocacy requires effort but unlocks enormous influence. Approach leaders as collaborative partners rather than adversarial gatekeepers. Blend compassion with courage to both humanize them and hold them accountable. Through patient preparation and persuasive framing, frontline wisdom gains power to transform enterprises for the better.

Aligning Expectations

Organizations run on coordinated effort enabled by leadership vision. The gap between envisioning strategy and executing operations requires bridging through aligned expectations. When priorities cascade clearly to frontlines and insights flow transparently to the top, fusion emerges propelling progress.

Mismatched expectations readily trigger disconnects resulting from differing perspectives across levels. Leaders obsessed with abstraction can misapprehend ground realities. At the same time, narrow functions overlook interdependencies and longer time horizons crucial for organization-wide coherence.

This complex interplay demands managing up to lead executives as much as down to direct operations. A two-way street underpins collective advancement where both sides navigate towards mutual destination. The following guide examines dynamics shaping senior leader expectations and techniques for productive alignment.

Why Alignment Matters

Nearly two-thirds of employees report lacking clear direction from management amidst already high ambiguity. Such disconnection breeds frustration and attrition from misapplied effort. Unfocused organizations neither inspire best work nor retain top talent.

Conversely, a study by Zenger Folkman found employees who believe leadership expectations were reasonable show extraordinarily higher commitment levels. Those given clear goals exceeded them over 70% of the time. Inspiration awakens dedication rather than dutiful drudgery.

Beyond intrinsic rewards, direct financial impacts result from expectation alignment. A Watson Wyatt study concluded companies with disciplined execution of defined goals generate returns nearly three times higher than undisciplined groups. Leadership and workforce pulling together in the same direction compounds capability.

For organizations navigating market complexity, internal coherence determines competitiveness. Aligned expectations enable responding in unison to dynamic opportunities and disruptive threats. Chaotic attempts at transformation will continue confusing. The path forward necessitates unified visions.

Where Misalignments Occur

Donald Sull termed the gap between leadership plans and field realities "the last mile problem." Even with perfect strategy, eventual outcomes depend on cascaded execution across intermediaries ultimately accountable for driving results. Intent deteriorates into wishful thinking without this final mile traversed.

Fractures appear within organizations through multiple mechanisms. The vision articulated at the top differs from interpretations by middle managers before final dissemination to customer facing employees. Further fragmentation creeps in from siloed departments and scattered geographies.

Nobel laureate Daniel Kahneman's seminal work on cognitive biases explains additional traps exacerbating disconnects. Leaders inhabit a distinctly different domain of abstract optimization relative to tangible day-to-day operations. Coupled with overconfidence in their expertise, skepticism regarding contradictory opinions takes hold.

Bridging the Divide

Progress depends on recognizing multiple legitimate perspectives while anchoring to organizational purpose. Though seeing the same reality differently, all stakeholders share common objectives. Arriving at truth requires welcoming disconfirming data without defensive posturing.

Emphasize communication frequency over perfection. Initial exchanges primarily scope the playing field allowing subsequent iterations to drive clarity. Neither confuse activity with alignment nor assume transparency from expressed agreements. Continually cross-check interpretations to determine genuine mindmeld building collective momentum.

The leader holds responsibility for driving disciplined execution around defined priorities. But guiding large groups through uncertainty equally demands humility regarding limitations of foresight. Instill confidence while inviting dialogue toNormalization of Deviance continually recalibrate direction. through curiosity, candor and courage.

Establishing Clear Purpose

Vectoring organizations to purposeful outcomes begins by defining the intended destination. Leaders must delineate an ambitious future vision together with supporting milestones marking progress along the journey to catalyze action in the present.

Where do we strive to reach as an organization? What guideposts determine if we are on track to getting there? Grounding in bold aspiration with believable pathway commitments focuses effort and resources towards targeted impacts. Abstract visions turn achievable when detailed with clear evolutionary leaps ultimately aggregating to the goal.

For instance, a non-profit seeking improved literacy rates in their county could set a 10 year objective to lift reading proficiency from current 60% to over 80% for third graders. Supporting milestones would establish incremental targets across years while outlining requisite budgeting for related tutoring programs, technology investments, teacher training and policy changes.

This sketches a roadmap for teams to orient priorities keeping the destination in sight. It allows locating current reality relative to the path ahead rather than wandering aimlessly. Leaders instill purpose by painting a vivid envisioned future together with feasible stepping stones to inspire progress.

Defining Mutual Needs

Alignment requires examining expectations flowing both up and down organizational structures. Leaders seek certain conditions and outputs from teams corresponding to assumptions around optimal decisions and success metrics.

But executives equally owe stakeholders upstream consultation, candid assessments, and empathetic listening. Leaders must discern team challenges, debate tradeoffs, and rework timelines keeping political and emotional realities in perspective.

A bank undergoing systemic changes held assumption-testing dialogues between executives spearheading the transformation and branch managers tasked with implementation. The initial feasibility assessments severely underestimated transition complexity and customer confusion.

Revelations from open conversations readjusted executive expectations on feasible speed while improving their support helping branch staff navigate turmoil. Collectively they redesigned communication plans and revised technology rollout phases. This constructive exchange governed ongoing adaptations enabling incremental optimization.

Results require responsibility flowing both ways. Leaders owe teams inspirational standards, developmental stretch and trusting empowerment. But guiding large systems through choppy waters equally demands responsiveness from helm based on currents only visible on deck. Progress quickens through mutually accountable expectations.

Tracking Accountability

Aligned expectations lose meaning without accountability given ever present temptations for prioritization creep and deadline slippage. Leaders in one study estimated over 80% compliance to their set targets though actual performance languished under 40% - a doubles disconnect reflecting wishful thinking unsupported by evidence.

Instill discipline through consistency - subordinates emulate priorities demonstrated by superiors rather than pronouncements alone. Reward delivery tied back explicitly to defined goals rather than effort proxy. Audit periodically but objectively avoiding emotions from interim shortfalls.

Cisco's use of recurring alignment reviews provides a template for expectation hygiene. The entire leadership annually presents priorities receiving CEO signoff before traveling globally to personally disclose plans. This sets the vision cascading through subsequent check-ins to confirm sustained consensus down chains of command.

Reliable achievement depends on shared benchmarks, independent tracking and routine reconciliation. Overcommunication breeds clarity on who owns what for when. Smooth the path by removing obstacles but verify outcomes to uphold mutual promises underpinning collective success.

Pursuing ambitious goals challenges organizational harmony requiring visions transcending limitations of current reality. Progress emerges through coordinated energy when executives paint an aspirational yet accessible future. Their role extends beyond issuing top-down orders to actively shepherding teams towards shared purpose.

With investment in sustained transparency, leaders manifest trust and progress. They focus on addressing disconnects not assigning blame. Results speak louder than rhetoric with evidence driving adaptations for advancement. By perpetually reexamining expectations both ways, organizations turn vision into unified velocity.

Key Takeaways and Final Thoughts on Working with Senior Management

Key Takeaways:

- Working with Senior Management requires understanding their strategic outlook and approach to complex problems driven by ambiguity and interdependence. Align recommendations to financial impacts using evidence tailored to their metrics.

- Gaining the executive perspective means appreciating the higher level view focused on cross-functional implications and long-term horizons. Learn to frame observations connected to broader competitive contexts.

- Senior leaders tackle interconnected portfolios of problems balancing multiple dynamic variables. Support through flexible analysis fused with intuitive judgement rather than linear recommendations.

- Influencing leadership demands clear communication grounded in empathy, transparency and solutions-orientation. Quantify ideas focused on organizational returns while welcoming scrutiny.

- Managing senior expectations involves ongoing dialogue, clearly defined incremental milestones, and mutual accountability structures tracking progress. Maintain trust by upholding candor.

Bridging Perspectives Across the Organization

Hierarchy inherently introduces perception gaps within enterprises based on differing priorities at each level. But organizations only unlock potential when information streams bidirectionally enabling decision quality through shared truths rather than isolated assumptions.

While responsibilities vary, collective orientation towards customer value harmonizes efforts. Structures must fuel transparency not obstruct it. As leadership sets direction, mid-level cross-functional integration translates strategy into operational realities. Frontlines closest to market forces feed insights up the chain.

Progress depends on inquisitive information flow not just top-down decrees. Executives must proactively seek countering views checking theories against ground sentiments. Equally, employees owe sharing full context including constraints to anchor leadership's aerial strategies.

With empathetic investigation of each other's reality, misperceptions clarifying into collaborative purpose. Leadership resolves through fusing lenses rather than imposing preferences. By perpetually reexamining divergent data points, strategy continually recalibrates towards dynamic opportunities.

The resulting interplay between hierarchical perspectives manifests organizational nimbleness. Lofty visions are made achievable by bridging the divides between abstraction and actuality. What integrates the levels also enables the enterprise.

Chapter Ten

Managing Upwards

The concept of "managing up" has become increasingly prevalent in leadership discourse over the past decade. Traditional notions of management portray a top-down, command-and-control structure in which managers solely direct the work of subordinates. However, the modern workplace requires a more collaborative ethos between managers and employees. Leading upwards encompasses a mindset rooted in mutual understanding, clear communication, and shared goals between both parties. When properly enacted, this approach benefits all involved by streamlining workflows, unlocking innovation, and nurturing interpersonal bonds.

At its core, leading upwards is not about manipulation or placation. Rather, it represents a willingness to understand a manager's strengths, weaknesses, working style and objectives. With this insight, an employee can better align their contributions for maximal productivity. They can utilize communication formats their manager best responds to, whether that involves succinct emails, informal check-ins, or structured performance reviews. They can also adopt working patterns complementary to the manager's own habits. If the manager tends to start work early, the employee can shift their schedule to enable collaboration at key junctions. Through simple adjustments like these, both sides mold around each other for smoother coordination.

The advantages of this approach are multifold. The manager enjoys greater output and reliability from reporting employees. With a grasp of individual working styles and preferences, they can better delegate responsibilities by aligning talent with appropriate tasks. The open communication minimizes misunderstandings which hamper timelines and morale. By leading upwards, the employee also accrues benefits. They gain a more receptive manager who acknowledges their effort and provides developmental support. Enhanced visibility of work and closer coordination secures fair performance assessment and faster career progression. The collaborative environment fosters essential soft skills like emotional intelligence, negotiation and conflict resolution.

While leading upwards produces mutual returns, enacting it does require some forethought. It is unreasonable to expect employees to understand managers innately without some background knowledge. Profiling techniques can be useful to discern aspects like working style, decision-making patterns and forms of appreciation. HR departments may provide guidance here by sharing manager profiles with new hires. Regardless employees should conduct some research themselves beforehand through informal conversations with team members.

Once an understanding is gained, certain principles enable upward leadership. Maintaining frequent, clear communication avoids situations where managers feel ignored or undermined. Providing early visibility into upcoming projects allows them to caliberate workstreams. Seeking honest feedback signals openness to improvement. Employees should also communicate personal career goals so managers can nourish professional development. Above all, leading upwards requires emotional self-regulation even in frustrating situations. Reactivity or criticism erodes the interpersonal fabric needed for functional relationships.

While traditional management paradigms still dominate, pockets of innovation recognize the need for flatter, cooperative structures. The holacracy model grants employees autonomy to self-organize around work. Agile methodologies empower project teams to collaboratively design workflows. These emerging frameworks may warrant full-scale adoption as globalization necessitates nimbler, human-centric enterprises. For now, however, leading upwards presents employees an immediate chance to cultivate mutual understanding despite structural constraints. The onus lies with individuals to nurture these interpersonal bonds across organizational divides.

Managing Your Manager

The dynamic between bosses and their staff plays an integral yet often overlooked role in determining organizational outcomes. While formal hierarchies portray a clear power differential, the reality proves more complex. In truth, both parties depend deeply on each other to accomplish their objectives. Employees rely on managers to provide strategic direction, resource allocation and career development. Meanwhile managers need staff to translate strategy into tangible results. Neither succeeds without the other's contributions. Yet this interdependence breeds natural tensions given the unequal roles. Ultimately through ongoing effort and understanding, both sides can transform inherent tensions into complementary working styles.

Employees in particular stand to gain from nurturing this relationship. Those who invest in fully comprehending their boss's expectations and adapt accordingly reap both personal and professional rewards. They become trusted advisors who earn greater developmental support. They also build transferable skills in areas like communication, empathy and conflict resolution. However doing so requires confronting certain assumptions that impede progress.

Rethinking Outdated Perspectives

The first step entails rethinking simplistic views of managers as all-knowing directors. In reality, most bosses also face pressures from their own superiors and operate with imperfect information. While responsible for their team's output, they cannot personally ensure results without dedication from staff. This reinforces the need for collective over individual efforts.

Employees also should not view themselves as passive implementers of top-down directives. Modern organizations have flattened bureaucratic layers, granting staff more discretion over their specific workstreams. Both professional experience and emotional investment in projects also give employees insight into operational barriers. By proactively raising concerns and suggesting solutions, they empower managers to make better-informed decisions.

Finally, the employee-manager relationship should not be reduced transactional terms. An underlying psychological contract connects both far more deeply through shared aspirations for the organization and mutual career advancement. While rarely articulated explicitly, upholding this informal covenant engenders trust and cooperation. Breaching it corrodes working relationships often irreparably.

Reframing these outdated assumptions opens space for recasting employees as active shapers of managerial ties. Through concerted effort, they can transform tensions arising from hierarchy into mutually fulfilling and productive partnerships.

Decoding the Managerial Psyche

With a more realistic perspective established, employees must deepen understanding of individual managers by decoding their psyche. Every boss maintains distinct expectations shaped by personality, past experiences and leadership style. Subordinates interact through this lens whether consciously aware or not. Surfacing latent heuristics that drive managerial behavior illuminates avenues for tailoring conduct.

Diagnosing working style patterns represents a natural starting point. Some managers operate very systematically, scheduling extensive planning meetings and requiring detailed project frameworks. Others favor more agile approaches, refracting goals flexibly as new information emerges. Neither constitute objectively "right" ways of directing teams. Rather, identifying inclinations early helps employees synchronize around rhythms conducive for collaboration.

Personality profiling provides another useful diagnostic. Widening emotional intelligence helps disambiguate outbursts or criticism. An introverted boss prone to anxiousness may withdraw around large groups or react defensively to perceived slights. One with domineering tendencies might instinctively dismiss suggestions from below. Understanding temperamental triggers and tailoring interactions to reassure rather than threaten helps preserve working relationships during moments of friction.

Employees should also examine decision-making habits, which greatly impact team dynamics. Some managers tightly control information flows and issue top-down decrees. They risk fostering resentment and also remaining ignorant of operational realities. Others actively consult staff in shaping strategy, engendering collective ownership. Employees who comprehend where their boss falls on this spectrum can share input accordingly to aid choices or make peace with unilateralism.

This psychoanalysis requires drawing intelligence through both formal and informal channels. HR evaluations offer high level insights by documenting strengths, weaknesses and professional goals. Peers also provide critical context around interpreting certain behaviors based on past observations. Ultimately though, employees themselves must form direct assessments through empirical observation during everyday interactions.

Activating Upward Leadership

With their manager psychologically deconstructed, employees can shift focus to enacting targeted upward leadership. This process is not about flattering egos or blind obedience. Rather it requires judicious application of certain principles tailored to individual personalities and preferences. While exhausting every adaption falls beyond any one article, we review key tenets vital for most contexts.

Clear Communication

Few managerial irritants generate more frustration than ambiguous messages from below. Employees therefore must strive for exceptional communicative clarity oriented around audience, timing and goals. Because bosses juggle input from many channels, employees should declare purpose upfront using succinct framing: "I wanted to update you on Project X and confirm next steps for approval." After relaying details, explicitly close information loops to verify interpretations: "Based on our discussion, I will submit the proposal by Friday assuming no additional changes on your end. Please confirm."

Adaptability

Interactions may not always unfold smoothly despite best efforts. Emotions flare; decisions get delayed; bad news emerges unexpectedly. Effective upward leadership requires rolling with turbulent punches by meeting managers where they stand emotionally. If major changes alter agreed operating assumptions, employees should adopt the mindset of adaptable advisors rather than indignant subordinates: "I understand leadership now feels quarterly revenue targets were unrealistic given wider industry headwinds. Let's regroup on what revised goals we should submit for approval."

Support

Because employees share collective responsibility for organizational outputs, they serve as mutual stakeholders rather than isolated workstreams. During periods of intense activity like budget planning or campaign launches, employees should detect overflow demands taxing their boss through late emails or hurried speech. They can provide tangible support by handling ancillary tasks proactively: "I know this week is extremely hectic with the product release. Let me take point consolidating status reports from the various teams so you have one document for review."

Development

The informal contract binding bosses and employees revolves fundamentally around advancement. Managers expect dedicated supporttied directly tocareer mobility. Employees in turn rely on higher-ups to furnishsponsorship, visibility and strategicguidance required for progression. This symbiosis breaks downwhere development stalls, oftenprompting separation. Employees should therefore deliberatelystrengthen developmental bonds bysharing personal goals and seeking advice for advancement. Even if no immediate opportunities exist, the exercise signals commitmentand reminds managersof mutualaspirations.

While enacting upward leadership presents no panacea for dysfunctional dynamics, consciously employing these techniques has the potential for enormous positive change. Transforming inherent tensions into complementary partnerships Lifting constraints so all organizational members reachfull potential. The tools for enabling this evolution rest primordially with frontline change agents. For in hierarchy as in nature,the seed must split for the flower to emerge.

Aligning Your Goals with Your Manager's

Navigating modern organizations requires more than just exemplary individual performance. Professionals must also build sturdy bridges spanning hierarchical divides. This entails moving beyond siloed workstreams to actively collaborate with management. While managers provide strategic guidance and development opportunities, employees reciprocate through dedicated execution. Yet this interdependency breeds natural friction without conscious relationship management. Employees in particular should initiate outreach that transforms latent tensions into shared aspirations. Aligning personal advancement with managerial success cements mutual investment for collective advancement.

Understand Your Manager's Style

The first step in this alignment process entails analyzing your direct manager's modus operandi.

Every leader maintains a distinct operating style shaped by innate preferences and past experiences. Diagnosing these tendencies helps employees tailor interactions for maximal resonance. This decoding requires assessing core management dimensions like working patterns, motivational triggers and communication formats.

For example, some managers operate very systematically with extensive planning rituals, structured agendas and serial approvals. Others favor agile approaches, remaining open to new inputs that reshape objectives accordingly. Neither constitute universally "correct" methods. But identifying leanings early allows employees to mesh rhythms and expectations.

Personality profiling also provides critical insights. Understanding natural dispositions aids interpreting certain comments or behaviors. An outburst from a hot-tempered boss reflects temperament rather than substance. Meanwhile, failure to acknowledge a contribution stems more from an introvert's discomfort with public affirmation than intentional slight. Spotting these motivational factors helps employees strengthen connections where they matter most to managers.

Communication habits also warrant examination given their centrality in workplace coordination. Some managers tightly control information sharing and decision deliberation. They issue top-down decrees with minimal explanation. Others actively consult staff in shaping strategy, fostering collective ownership through transparency. Employees who grasp where their boss falls along this spectrum can share input accordingly without misaligned and potentially counterproductive efforts.

Gleaning these observations requires amalgamating both formal evaluations like performance appraisals and informal observations during daily interactions. But direct empiricism ultimately provides the richest illustrations. Keeping detailed track of meetings, comments and emails builds an accurate managers profiling.

Align Weekly

With your manager's modus operandi mapped, focus turns to enacting behaviors that facilitate alignment.

Many tensions between employees and managers trace back to unclear, untimely or inconsistent communications that foster misunderstandings. Employees should therefore emphasize simple, straightforward and regular information sharing tailored around managerial preferences.

Scheduling brief weekly check-ins provides helpful guardrails for collaboration, especially for systematic managers who appreciate structured coordination. Come prepared with bullet point updates on recently completed projects, upcoming priorities requiring direction, and festering issues meriting intervention. Summarize key takeaways before closing to verify interpretations.

During periods of intense activity, double down on communication through more frequent but concise updates. Preemptively surface concerns before they escalate into problems so the manager can calibrate accordingly. Frame suggestions constructively around collective imperatives: "Acme account managers feel we need to reconsider this quarter's revenue target given wider industry conditions. Should we discuss reformulating what we submit for leadership approval?"

Outside formal interactions, copy managers on relevant emails or reports to reinforce information sharing. Drop by their office occasionally simply to touch base informally. These small but consistent actions enable managers to monitor workstreams closely without micromanaging. They simultaneously afford employees greater visibility for their effort and reliability.

Sweating the Small Stuff

Relationships with managers hinge profoundly on execution of seemingly mundane administrative tasks that keep operations flowing smoothly.

Managers juggle overflowing inboxes, crowded calendars and endless meetings while still overseeing strategy and employee development. Employees who alleviate such auxiliary burdens through proactive ownership of minor responsibilities create immense value disproportionate to the tasks themselves.

Maintaining meticulous personal organization aids significantly here. From critical deadlines like performance check-ins to routine team meetings, employees should master individual schedules and related deliverables. Submit requests well in advance of required turnaround rather than applying last minute pressure. Precompile statuses across workstreams before meetings rather than adding prep labor for managers. Handle ancillary analyses or data reconciliations that undergird recommendations without constant oversight.

Such conscientiousness earns credibility gradually as managers come to rely on an employee's autonomous handling of essential basics. It also signals commitment beyond narrow technical obligations. Staff who simply complete assigned tasks check a box. Those who proactively govern ancillary workflow knots without prompting demonstrate investment in collective outcomes.

Cultivating such horizontal leadership is neither quick nor linear. But over time, the compounding effect of small courtesies builds bonds of affinity and loyalty whose collective strength far outweighs any individual strand.

Tethering Trajectories

At its core, the employee-manager relationship revolves around advancement.

Managers expect dedicated support and execution from staff which directly enables their own success. Employees in turn rely on bosses to furnish the sponsorship, visibility and strategic direction essential for progression. This symbiotic investment falls apart where either side feels stalled professionally. Employees should therefore deliberately nurture developmental links by sharing personal goals transparently and seeking active guidance from managers.

Annual reviews provide natural junctions for this trajectory mapping through documented plans and evaluation feedback. But informal check-ins better support persistent nudges. Occasionally highlight accomplishments from recent projects and how they strengthened your skills. Float aspirations for skills development or innovative roles that leverage untapped talents. Outline how envisaged growth synergizes with group objectives for added resonance.

Not every manager can furnish immediate promotion opportunities. But the simple exercise signals hunger for challenge and stimulates reciprocal reflection on alignments between individual employees and team imperatives. Over time, even modest career steps compound expanding possibilities for both sides. More importantly, the process itself cements bonds between levels through a shared language of aspiration and advancement.

While managers oversee operations, employees ultimately constitute the gears turning strategy into tangible results. Recognition of this interdependence is the first step towards transforming latent tensions into productive partnerships. Employees in particular should initiate outreach across hierarchical divides by first comprehending managerial expectations, then adapting behaviors accordingly. Small consistent investments to facilitate leadership eventually produce outsized returns in trust, visibility and support. In hierarchy as in nature, seeds must crack for blossoms to bloom.

Advocating for Your Team and Projects

Innovation and execution form two halves of the organizational machinery driving enterprise forward. Senior executives craft bold visions to sharpen competitive positioning and expand market share. Frontline employees furnish insights that transform high-level frameworks into tangible outputs reflecting operational constraints. Yet a gulf often yawns between strategic aspiration and ground realities. Middle managers play an indispensable role bridging this divide as conduits, synthesizing heterogeneous perspectives across levels to enrich decisions. They advocate for resources that empower teams while aligning local imperatives with organization-wide objectives. Mastering this upward advocacy unlocks capabilities for both employees and institutional leaders.

Connecting Across the Hierarchy

Advocacy flows most persuasively from comprehension - in this case, grasping executive outlooks. Senior manager perspectives diverge markedly from employee views given differentiated mandates. Executives concern themselves with long-term value creation, growth cultivation and shareholder returns. They scan the competitive horizon for pantheon opportunities while relying on teams below to govern executional complexities. These lofty and expansive objectives shape certain heuristics when evaluating proposals from frontline units.

Understanding these instincts is vital for middle managers aiming to secure executive buy-in. When approaching senior leadership, ground recommendations in financial return projections, benchmarking data and tangible competitive advantages. Package suggestions around addressing organizational pain points flagged in shareholder communiques. Link ideas directly to corporate vision statements already endorsed as strategic goals. The more logically a case syncs with accepted priorities, the higher its chance of adoption.

This translation exercise also applies when navigating individual personalities. Decision makers respond differently based on intuitive preferences even when governed by the same institutional agenda. Some prize bold innovation; others prefer incremental change secured through meticulous planning. Tailor cases to leverage personal tendencies already observed through past interactions. Lead with big picture impact for visionaries; dive into details on resource utilization for operationally minded pragmatists.

No foolproof formula guarantees endorsement. But wherever possible, couch arguments in language that resonates across hierarchical divides.

Spotlighting Contributions

Beyond particular proposals, fundamental perceptions of team relevance also hinge on visible contributions to corporate objectives. Middle managers play lead broadcasters role here, trumpeting group accomplishments so they register on executive radar. Consistent signaling spotlights frontline efforts otherwise obscured from the strategic apex by layers of bureaucracy.

Various communications channels should funnel upwards evidence demonstrating group efficacy and alignment with organizational goals. Monthly status briefings represent natural conduits for rattling off recent wins tracked against targets. Client testimonials and public reviews make immense impact given executive fixation on external brand perception. Even informal conversations should artfully highlight team impacts: "The Australia launch materials prepared by my product designers received rave feedback from partners, who said our polish far outpaces competitors."

This amplification role extends beyond direct superiors to diverse organizational stakeholders. Laterally networked messages ensure wide acknowledgement across leadership of unique team excellence. They also furnish executive backers external validation to aid internal sponsorship efforts for team initiatives needing support. Credibility compounds gradually over time as consistent signaling cuts through inherent information barriers between headquarters and the field.

When combined with a sound understanding of executive outlooks, spotlighting thus enables tailored communications that resonate with priority audience. It transforms middle managers into trusted advisors who proactively link frontline observations with strategic considerations.

Tethering Task Forces

Middle managers' most invaluable service comes through tying localized contributions to big picture imperatives that ultimately drive decisions. Tenacious advocacy therefore requires framing team goals as fulfilling rather than competing with organizational visions.

Several communication techniques help facilitate reconciliation between local and enterprise aims. Where possible, directly incorporate senior leadership feedback into team planning cycles. Treat advice as precious intelligence on shifting priorities to structurally embed within operations rather than merely paying lip service outwardly. Granular decomposition of corporate five year plans provides helpful reverse engineering blueprints. Rerun this strategic filtering with any new group objective or task effort that emerges to guarantee tight alignment.

Additionally, evaluate team aspirations through an institutional productivity lens by showcasing process enhancements that unlock wider efficiencies. Does distributing certain technical functions across business units boost scale and resilience or maintain risky redundancies? Do proposed digital upgrades streamline internal coordination or primarily help external marketing? Addressing these tensions openly spotlights the expansive benefits conferred beyond narrow team boundaries.

Finally, actively socialize solutions cross-functionally to gather lateral buy-in before advocating upwards for funding. Test cases with peer groups reveal potential executional blind spots, strengthen viable options through collective input and widen future endorsement coalitions. Justifies particularly precious investments require slow deliberate coalition expansion to cement durable supports - a wise investment before braving senior executive scrutiny.

Emphasize Achievements, Acknowledge Challenges

Advancing arguments grounded in team contributions requires equal parts spotlighting achievements and honestly assessing deficiencies. Celebrate group accomplishments consistently but avoid self-congratulatory excess. Where possible, source external validation through client feedback, peer acknowledgement or formal benchmarks. On challenges, resist performative overpromising aimed primarily at self-preservation. Own setbacks transparently while outlining constructive responses that address systemic gaps.

Balancing this duality sustains a realistic yet aspirational tone when engaging leadership. It foregrounds positive momentum fueled by a hunger for continual improvement rather than defensive fragility. As trust solidifies over successive interactions, the candor crucial for accurately diagnosing institutional limitations flows more freely. But middle managers should walk the talk first, demonstrating receptiveness towards criticism in handling of their own team's performance.

By holding a mirror to group capabilities - blinded spots included - middle managers manifest their pivotal role reconciling external assessments with internal capabilities for senior leaders struggling to connect between lofty visions and on-the-ground realities. These should be continual conversations rather than one-off appeals, strengthening alignment through understanding built gradually in both directions.

Institution Building Beyond Projects

Effective advocacy ultimately transcends particular proposals to instead nurture institutional resilience. Middle managers occupy an invaluable vantage bridging executive suites and operational trenches. As such, their highest purpose comes through sustainably transmitting cross-level intelligence to inform better decisions and reinforce cultural cohesion. They serve as lifelong ambassadors who guide organizational evolution based on demonstrated impacts over rhetoric.

While knocking on senior leadership doors when team needs arise may score short-term gains, only through lasting bridge building does transformation take root. No single project ever reflects narrow objectives pursued by isolated units. Each effort represents one strand in an interwoven tapestry either harmonized or frayed based on the strength of weaving in between by those who traverse organizational layers, connecting insights with imperatives that drive purposeful progress. It is here where middle managers either facilitate greatness or failure.

Key Takeaways and Final Thoughts on Managing Upwards

Key Takeaways:

- Modern organizations depend on seamless collaboration between strategic leaders who craft vision and frontline staff who furnish insights that transform vision into action. Middle managers play an indispensable role spanning divides by understanding and reconciling priorities across levels.

- Managing up builds sturdy upward ties through comprehending manager psychology and adapting behaviors accordingly. Small consistent investments - structured check-ins, visible reliability, developmental nudges - transform relationships over time.

- Aligning team goals with organizational imperatives signals value beyond narrow functions. Actively socialize solutions for peer input, directly incorporate leadership feedback into operations, and evaluate ideas on overall productivity gains.

- Spotlighting team accomplishments broadcasts relevance to senior executives while assessment of deficiencies shows receptiveness towards continuous improvement. Balance celebrating contributions with setting aspirational expectations.

- Sustainably effective advocacy requires moving from isolated appeals to serving as lifelong ambassadors transmitting intelligence across layers. The highest purpose comes through nurturing institutional resilience by connecting insights with strategic decisions.

Bridging the Cross-Boundary Leadership Divide

Modern enterprises operate as complex webs of interconnected teams, integrated yet separated across functions, geographies and hierarchies. Senior executives craft expansive visions steering competitive strategy. Customer-facing units furnish grounded insights revealing operational constraints. Everyone occupies a narrow role optimizing particular outputs.

Yet organizational potential exceeds the sum of individual contributions. Achieving excellence depends profoundly on integrating disparate efforts into synchronized flows aligned towards common goals. This integration relies on leadership able to traverse divides by comprehending varied motivations and reconciling differing priorities.

Middle managers inhabit a unique position bridging the gulf between strategic leaders and frontline realities. Through dedicated outreach, they transform inherent tensions arising from hierarchy into shared purpose and collaborative achievement. They advocate for resources that empower employees while aligning local imperatives with global objectives. They spotlight team accomplishments to senior executives while assessing internal deficiencies with candor to enable continuous improvement.

Most impactfully, effective middle managers serve as conduits synthesizing multifaceted inputs and flows across scattered channels into coherent wholes far greater than compartmentalized components. They personify the tissue integrating organizational nervous systems, transmitting signals between centers directing strategy and limbs executing operations. For it is connection, not isolation, that enables excellence.

The question before every middle manager then becomes: will I barricade myself within structural siloes or break open boundaries that obstruct communication flows vital for institutional thriving? Am I simply an employee or an institution builder who transcends the immediate to nurture the enduring? In hierarchy as in nature, seeds must crack for blossoms to bloom. And middle managers occupy the fertile common ground where falling barriers transform disconnected efforts into thriving ecosystems.

Chapter Eleven
Conclusion

We began this exploration by acknowledging the profound responsibilities conferred upon organizational leaders - whether formal executives or informal influencers - based on their capacity to shape collective outcomes through decisions and example. Followers entrust authority figures with irreplaceable talents, time and trust. Yet history furnishes disturbing reminders that dominance absent checks risks distortion of judgement and conduct.

Leadership demands diligent accountability. As we have seen throughout these chapters, realizing potential while upholding obligations depends profoundly on cultivating personal qualities of integrity and emotional intelligence blended fluidly with formal capabilities. Authority figures must grasp that their primary purpose lies in empowering teams to unlock ingenuity and chase dreams, not establishing personal preeminence. True leaders occupy elevated platforms solely to lift others higher.

Modern uncertainties underscore this imperative for wisdom. Technological disruptions continuously reshape competitive landscapes while social scrutiny keeps leaders under constant examination. In such a climate marked by volatility, complexity and ambiguity, no individual harbors sufficient expertise alone to guarantee outcomes. Progress depends profoundly on decentralizing decisions closest to emerging opportunities and integrating scattered insights across silos.

This forces a reckoning with dated paradigms of leadership as commanding supremacy over subordinate followers. Effectiveness now relies on galvanizing collective participation through inspirational influence more than formal authority. The leader's differentiating capability stacks upon personal credibility from expertise and accountability - establishing basic trust. But sustainable activation requires enrolling teams emotionally through framing projects as shared quests customized to intrinsic motivations while forging empathetic connections on individual levels.

Likewise, traversing divisions to synthesize perspectives and reimagine constraints unlocks innovation impossible through isolated efforts. Leaders must serve as conduits integrating flows and signaling possibilities rather than bottlenecking progress through control obsession. Negotiations transform from zero-sum transactions into open canvases for decentralized collaboration when influence wielders continuously expand perceived potential through integrative creativity.

Ultimately, organizational optimization depends profoundly on flattened architectures where senior strategists, middle managers and frontline teams operate in symmetric partnership rather than closed-loop silos. Progress manifests not through top-down decrees but rather lateral leadership fusing insights emerging from proximity to customers with vision originating from executive abstraction. The future favors learning nervous systems over rigid organs.

Therefore, the differentiating capability for modern leaders involves nurturing cultures that dissolve fears around uncertainty and error in themselves and colleagues. With foundations of psychological security established, creative passions flourish and teams transform tentative ideas into unleashed innovation. They dream not in isolation but cross-pollination.

The leader's craft centers on upholding an environment that replaces outdated habits of mistrust, coercion and self-interest with honestly human pillars: compassion, courage and collective ambition. And nothing so thoroughly reorients culture as leaders courageously examining and evolving their own behaviors first. Never demanding from teams what they fail to model personally around integrity, accountability and care.

Where does this analysis leave aspiring leaders seeking to implement insights across the contemporary challenges discussed? While prescribing universal solutions risks oversimplifying vastly diverse and perpetually dynamic contexts, several key takeaways furnish signposts for the journey ahead:

Redefine Leadership as Service

Rather than pursuing authority as a platform for personal elevation or benefit, reframe elevated roles solely as vehicles for empowering human and organizational progress. The underlying motive must focus on responsibility more than power. Ask constantly: "How can I spark potential in others?"

Customize Approaches

Acknowledge the multifaceted diversity across modern workforces and that singular models of inspiration fail to resonate uniformly. Observe individuals carefully to discern intrinsic motivations, values and sources of meaning. Then customize leadership approaches to connect authentically on personal levels. Mutuality matters more than uniformity.

Forge Connections

Progress depends profoundly on cooperation not control. Move beyond transactional interactions focused on immediate returns alone to intentionally build mutual understanding across the organization. Nurture relationships spanning formal boundaries and hierarchies. Leaders serve as neural hubs within ecosystems unified by trust.

Facilitate Understanding

The leader's essential function involves sensemaking - gathering, filtering and framing information to enable clarity amidst uncertainty for teams. Make asking thoughtful questions that illuminate reality a consistent priority over decree. And ensure visibility flows bidirectionally, seeking dissenting perspectives across hierarchies. Progress manifests through fused insight not isolated assumptions.

Reframe Constraints as Catalysts

When facing seemingly intractable hurdles related to resources, bureaucracy, outdated metrics or other apparent obstacles, avoid resignation or complaining. Such experiences furnish opportunities to question inherited limitations and collaborative reimagine possibility. Turn constraints into springboards through positive inquiry focused on integrative solutions.

Decentralize Innovation

While strategic leaders craft vision, sustainable transformation depends on mobilizing progress across the dispersed spectrum of the organization. Push decision autonomy around experimentation to frontlines closest to Customer needs and market changes. Empower creative collisions by architecting physical and digital systems supporting transparency, networking and information flows Laterally. Gather opinions expansively before determining direction.

Measure Holistically

Evolve metrics to assess collective advancement towards shared goals and customer value rather than simply monitoring narrow functional output. This prevents people from optimizing siloed productivity at cost to institutional mission. Evaluate decisions based on cross-organizational impact and strategic priorities beyond this quarter's budget.

Model Behaviors

Teams ultimately commit to initiatives they witness leaders themselves practicing consistently regarding integrity, vulnerability, empathy, accountability and passion. Rely on influence through idealized inspiration more than formal authority. Communications matter but actions outweigh words. If you find yourself expecting from others what you fail to prioritize personally first, consider what example calls for realignment.

Keep Growing

Mastery remains a horizon always beyond reach. Maintain perpetual humility in the face of ever-expanding complexity and promise of human progress. None of us occupy the apex of achievement alone but rather stand on the shoulders of giants before us. Consider leadership as an invitation to lifelong learning. Bring others along by sponsoring their development journeys as allies.

The insights presented across these pages aim to furnish signposts for readers navigating leadership contexts as empowered partners ready to expand possibility and propel dreams into reality. But the purpose stays not to dictate destinations or administer step-by-step guidance. Such rigid overcontrol risks the very dysfunctions we have unpackede throughout this analysis.

Instead, the concepts explored seek to orient leaders towards the broader opportunity and obligation before us - catalyzing human potential into cooperative creation through morally imaginative influence, not fear-based coercion. And every organization offers a rich canvas for expressing unique gifts and passions while advancing institutional purpose.

Therefore, may the insights herein inspire a reexamination of assumptions about traditional notions of leadership, hierarchy and purpose that open new frontiers. Now equipped with expanded mental models, where will you lead differently moving forward? What once seemed static now awaits reimagination.

Stewarding progress constitutes sacred work. But the resultant rewards of unlocking ingenuity and purpose across human beings promise returns beyond quantification - the actualization of collective possibility into bold new futures benefitting whole communities. That ultimately must stand as leadership's highest aim.

When we lift each other, how high might we soar together? Now, let's get started...